Richard
Wurmbrand

A VOICE IN
THE
DARK

by Catherine
Mackenzie

Christian Focus Publications

B
Wurmbrand

T-26932

© 1997 Catherine Mackenzie
ISBN 1-85792-298-0

Published in 1997 by Christian Focus Publications Ltd,
Geanies House, Fearn, Tain, Ross-shire,
IV20 1TW, Scotland, Great Britain
Reprinted 1998, 2000

 **CHRISTIAN FOCUS**

Cover design by Owen Daily
Cover illustration by N Burgin
Printed and bound in Great Britain by
Cox and Wyman, Cardiff Road, Reading

*****
Note to the reader
The people in this story are real people and the things
that happen to them in this book actually took place.
However, some of the conversations have been created
by the author, but are based on the true life experiences
of Richard Wurmbrand.

 is a registered trademark of The Voice of the Martyrs, Inc.
and may not be reproduced in whole or in part in any form
without written consent of The Voice of the Martyrs, Inc.
Used by permission.

Contents

11-9-05 $5.99

Arresting Times

A young man strides out across the city street, his long brown overcoat flapping in the breeze. There is nobody to talk with him this evening. He walks alone. But he talks with God.

'Father, thank you for this beautiful evening. The sunshine, the warmth, the fresh breeze. Thank you for the warmth of your love to me, for the fresh breeze of the Holy Spirit on my heart. Your ways are wonderful.'

He hums quietly to himself. A hymn tune comes to mind as he strides along over the dry, cracked paving-stones.

Suddenly, a crowd of young shining faces appear from out of an imposing red doorway. They march towards him. Heels hitting the concrete, they push past the young man. No more singing. His hymn is silent now.

The crimson red scarves seem to shout from across the busy street – '*We are the Communist[1] youth. We are the future. There is no God. We are the future.*'

The young man sighs. He walks on. He was one of them ... once.

He mutters under his breath, 'I too was a believer in lies.'

The young man's Sunday shoes stride out again over the cracked paving-stones.

A barrage of noise and colour meet him as he passes by the market stalls. Traders shout out to passers-by trying desperately to sell their last few vegetables. Bright

---

1. Communism – Political belief that all goods should be the property of the community.

red peppers and green lettuce sit on one stall, the lovely aroma of home-made bread wafts out from behind another. People shout out to the young man as he rushes past.

'Fresh fruit. Fresh vegetables. Come and buy. Come and buy. Delicious. Very, very delicious.'

The young man turns and smiles, adding ' ... and very, very, expensive? Yes?'

The stall-holder pauses, and smiles back. 'Expensive yes, but you will not get these vegetables any cheaper in the whole of Romania – no, not in the whole of the Communist World.'

The young man laughs as the trader turns to persuade a young woman to buy the very expensive lettuces. Cars and chatter, music and laughter are just part of the hustle and bustle of the city preparing to shut up shop for another day.

A neighbour cries out over the garden fence, 'Jacob, is your mother's cough any better this evening?'

A young mother gently whispers to her child, 'Sergei, mother loves you. Be a good boy and come in for your supper.'

A laughing young girl skips along the pavement singing about 'Love.'

The young man longs for freedom of speech.

'If I was allowed to speak freely Lord, I would tell that young girl about you – the Creator of Love. At least Lord, the Communists cannot read my mind – my thoughts are still my own. Lord make them more like your thoughts.'

The Sunday shoes weave in and out avoiding other Sunday shoes going in other directions.

Nobody's eyes meet. All eyes look down. Today is a risk. A battle of wits. You hold your breath in on days like this. Your shoulders shrink down and you ignore everybody else. Hopefully everybody else will ignore you. The young man sighs, 'Worshipping God is not something to be ashamed of. But the Communists make loving God a crime!'

He longs to turn to the tired mother, the young daughter, the little child – just to say the most beautiful words in the world –

'*JESUS LOVES YOU*!'

But these words are banned.

Red scarves do not allow.

Communists and their youth do not permit.

But sometimes a whisper is heard and the joy of Jesus is passed on. His voice is a voice in the dark. An urgent whisper, a warning.

The young man's whispers have touched hearts. His shouts have woken others from death. He has passed on Jesus Christ as if he were hot coals. That gets noticed. That is not ignored. The young man's steps are being counted. The Sunday shoes striding out across the cracked paving stones are being watched.

'A few more strides and I will be in sight of the meeting house. Time enough for a quiet moment with Jesus before the service begins.'

Five more strides and he is round the corner.

Black car.

Screech of tyres.

Black rubber against grey concrete.

Slamming doors.

Screeching tyres.

The young man is swallowed up as grasping arms, iron hand-cuffs and frantic shoves pin him down.

Richard Wurmbrand. Arrested by the People's Government of Romania.

***

'Where am I? What are you doing? Where are you taking me?' Richard's voice cracked under the strain. His heart was pounding, he could hardly breathe. Gasping for air he realised – This was the nightmare!

Thoughts kept coming quick and fast, so much so, he could hardly make sense of anything.

'I must keep control.' Richard spoke out loud.

An evil chuckle broke out from beside him, 'You are no longer in control. We are your worst nightmare!'

'Am I a prisoner? Is this an arrest?'

The Secret Police are silent and don't even bother to reply.

Panicking slightly Richard tried to make sense of the situation.

'Of course this is an arrest. What else can it be? Grabbed off the street in broad daylight! Shoved into an unmarked police car. Driven off at high speed. Look at their eyes, one minute hot with rage the next cold with emptiness. I am just an object to them. They treat me like dung! God's family are treated worse than dung.'

Sweat poured off Richard's forehead. His arms were pinned down hard against the back seat of the car. He couldn't even wipe away the sweat that trickled down his nose and into his eyes.

The tyres screeched again as the car turned sharply round the next corner.

Houses, schools and church buildings all passed by on the outside. The people running around on the pavements had no idea what was going on inside the speeding black car.

Richard couldn't help but worry about his family. Plucking up some courage he turned to the guard on his right, 'I have a wife and son. What are they going to do?'

The guard sneering, turned to Richard and screamed, 'Prisoner! Be quiet! That is an order. It is not permitted for you to speak unless you are under direct order to do so!' Richard turned away to face the front of the vehicle. He did not want to look in their faces.

'I will definitely not ask any more questions.' Richard let his thoughts turn to the sermon he would no longer preach that evening. But he could not avoid sneaking a look at the clenched fists of the armed guards beside him. Heavy truncheons hung limply from their belt buckles. Richard battled to keep the tears of pain and fear under check. He had little enough control of his life at the moment. He was not going to give in to his own fear.

'Lord, help me.'

The car tyres screeched again as they turned onto a street called 'Calea Rahova'. The street sign was just visible out of the murky window. Steel gates opened onto a large court yard and Richard realised he had finally arrived at his destination. This would be his home for the immediate future.

The gates started to creak as they were drawn shut on the outside world. Richard quickly turned round to take what would be his last look at the outside world for quite some time.

'When will I be able to walk out in that world again? The free world ...'

The doors opened and Richard was shunted from one world into another. One fist punched his back from behind, another boot kicked his shin. The guards frogmarched Richard across the courtyard and through a grey door on the other side. The metal doors clanged behind him and Richard was ordered to stand still and say nothing.

Efficient, cold hands stripped off his belongings, his clothes, his identity and his freedom. Hands quickly and efficiently removed Richard Wurmbrand the pastor and replaced him with Vasile Georgescu, the unknown, the unwanted. One in a thousand. To be used and disposed of as quickly and as quietly as possible. Richard's life, his name, his whole identity lay on the floor in a pile along with his notes, his Bible, his tie and shoelaces.

Prisoner, March!

'Prisoner, March!'

The prisoner marched.

'Keep moving, keep moving! Stop loitering Georgescu!' Richard felt strange being called that but even the prison officers did not know who they were dealing with. The prison authorities had removed Richard's identity so completely that nobody knew who he was. The Communists considered it vital that Richard's identity remained hidden. Nobody, not even Richard's wife was to know where he was.

Voices shouted in Richard's ear as he stumbled along dimly lit corridors. A sack had been placed over his head. He could see nothing and no-one.

'What don't they want me to see?' he wondered.

They turned round another corner and Richard felt the fist in his back again.

'Move along Georgescu – MOVE! NOW!'

It was always shouts, sharp words and frantic movements. Richard had no idea where he was.

Then it hit him – that was why he had the bag over his head. 'I could never find my way out of this prison without getting totally lost.'

Out of nowhere an arm yanked him back and the sound of scratching metal against metal told Richard that another key was being turned in another lock. The bag was lifted off his face and Richard looked in a door – the first of many doors that he would not be able to open.

This door signalled a new beginning. This was an end to the free life he had led before. This cell was his new life. Richard stepped inside his new life.

'Ah!' Richard exclaimed. 'I will thank the Lord for my blessings. I have a window!'

A small window let some light in from high up the prison wall. The small square let warm rays of sunshine into the cold chill of the prison garrison. Richard stood and tried to let its warmth permeate into his cold body.

'It was such a beautiful warm day today. Now I am shivering. It is as if all the hate in this place has frozen it.'

Looking around him he noticed two wooden plank beds, one on either side of the cell. Richard sat down on one and waited.

He sighed and decided to try and look out the window. Standing up he found he was quite tall enough to get a good view out onto the courtyard below.

Chuckling to himself he thought about all the times he had wished he had shorter legs.

'All those times in bed when my feet stuck out the other end. I used to wish they would make a bed especially measured for me.' Richard took a deep breath.

'I must prepare myself. There is one thing I am 100% sure of. In a Communist Romanian prison you are not just here to fill a cell. The Secret Police want to know something. My secrets, others' secrets. My sins, others' sins. There will be no privacy – just questions, questions, questions. And that will be just the beginning. That will just be the interrogation.'

Sitting back again on the plank bed Richard made his mind face the awful prospect of what was bound to come.

'There may be torture.'

Bowing his head Richard prayed to his father in heaven.

'I may even die.'

An aching plea to his beloved creator was heard and answered.

Richard's thoughts wandered from his dark prison cell. His mind escaped from the present and went back to his past.

***

'Ah, hello there – it is little Richard Wurmbrand. A fine little boy you are.'

The old man turned to the church elder beside him and muttered, 'Such a shame, their father died when he was only nine years old. His family is always short of money – I am sure this child even goes hungry.'

'We should do something for them,' replied the grey-suited church elder.

'I am going to buy the young man a suit next weekend. We will go to the merchant's together. Nothing too grand, but something presentable.'

Richard smiled, a new suit was a grand thing. He didn't know the last time he had got a new suit. His mother couldn't afford one. They were so poor.

The next weekend Richard and the man went to the store to look at suits. Walking in through the door the bell clanged to announce the arrival of another potential customer.

'Ah, good afternoon Sir, and how can I help you this fine day?'

The assistant smiled warmly at what was obviously

quite a well-off customer.

'I am looking for a suit for this young gentleman here.'

The assistant looked down at the slightly worse-for-wear young gentleman, smiled and said, 'Why, I have just the thing. If you will come this way we can let the young gentleman try it on through the back.'

Fluttering her way through the back the assistant returned with a well-made, presentable young man's suit. It was by far the best that they had on offer.

Richard smiled. The suit looked good.

The older man drew in his breath. Sucking his teeth he said, 'Far too good for this boy!'

The tone of the voice, the rejection, stayed with Richard all his life.

***

The prisoner came back momentarily from his memories. Yes, God had helped him even before he knew of God's existence. Richard thought about the young child who read every book he could get his hands on but who could hardly afford to get a new coat for winter.

'Poverty made things very hard for our young family,' thought Richard. 'My mother had a difficult job keeping food on the table. But thankfully one thing that we did have was lots of books. Books were everywhere – on shelves, in cupboards, propped up on a window sill or more often than not propped up between two boyish hands. Thank you, God, for looking after your little child. You cared about me, about my thirst for knowledge. Even when I read that you didn't exist and even when I believed it – you still cared about me.'

Richard Wurmbrand had mentally devoured every

book in the house – good and bad – before he was ten years old.

The prisoner drifted back to the past.

'It's so good to look back and see God's hands directing me – even as a little child I had an interest in religion...'

***

'What's that man saying? I can't make him out.'

Richard was sitting in the local synagogue twiddling his thumbs a little as the service was drawing to a close. Brought up in a Jewish family, Richard was accustomed to attending the old dark brown building. The scriptures would be read and prayers would be said to the all-seeing God, but this morning Richard was especially listening to a prayer being uttered just a row or two down from him. The man was praying and tears were flowing down his cheeks.

'Why is he crying?' Richard couldn't understand what the problem was.

Listening harder he caught hold of a few words,

'Please heal my child, save my little girl. Yahweh[1], don't let her die. Have mercy and heal her.'

Richard saw the pain in the man's face. You heard it in his voice.

'Will God heal her?' Richard wondered. Richard doubted. Richard waited to see if this so-called God would actually do anything to heal the little girl.

'Will he or won't he?' he pondered.

The next day Richard heard that the little girl had died. Richard could not understand. He had so many questions, but no answers.

---

1. Yahweh – the name of God which indicates he makes promises to bless his people.

He asked the Rabbi[2], 'What God could refuse such a desperate prayer?'

The Rabbi had no answer.

'God can't be all-powerful when so many people are hungry, ill, suffering. And as for this Jesus – I don't believe in him either.'

The young Richard Wurmbrand angrily turned away from all thoughts of God. God would no longer be included in any part of Richard Wurmbrand's life.

***

Richard looked at the four prison walls.

'Well, God, I didn't know it but I was in prison then. My soul was so tied up in sin and unbelief. God – not knowing you, not believing that you even existed – it was like having chains around my heart, but I didn't feel them. I just went on in my own way. But you were there waiting for that moment – that glorious moment when you would make me yours – I took my time about it though, didn't I? I must have been twenty-five or more before you decided enough was enough and it was time I came to my senses...'

Richard grimaced as he remembered what kind of a man he had been at twenty-five – well-off, successful, keen to enjoy all that the pubs and night life of Bucharest had to offer...

***

'Richard, which club are we going to tonight?,' a workmate called out to him from across the office.

'Oh, I don't know, how about that one next to the square, the one with the dancing girls?'

---

2. Rabbi – Jewish teacher.

Richard laughed as all the young men whooped in anticipation at yet another Friday night of drinking and dancing. They left their offices at five o'clock, meeting up with other young businessmen on the way. Another night of rowdy entertainment was theirs to enjoy. Many people looked at the young men and women hanging around the bars and nightclubs and envied them. Richard had it all – or so they thought.

One thing Richard didn't have was peace of mind.

Standing beside another drink of beer, arm around the waist of another young woman, Richard couldn't understand exactly what it was that was bothering him.

'I have everything that I ever wanted. Look at yourself man, what more is there? You have enough money to keep yourself fed, clothed and very adequately entertained.'

Richard paused in his thoughts to laugh at somebody's joke which really wasn't very funny anyway. But that was his life – it was a con. Everything he did and said was just another act in a stupid film.

'I go about from day to day living a life that has no meaning, that is full of rubbish, worth nothing.'

People milled about, shouting and laughing. The young woman had moved away to someone who was more attentive – she had got bored of the dull, depressing young man.

Richard stared at the bottom of his glass.

'I know that there is no God, I am sure of it. But I wish there was. Deep down in my heart I wish God really did exist. I might have a reason to live then ... that would be good!'

Swallowing the last drop from the glass, Richard

turned and looked at his friends enjoying themselves. Signalling to one of the boys from the office he shouted across the din of the busy nightclub.

'I'm off. Don't feel too good. I'll see you Monday!'

'O.K. Richard, Monday! I'll have a hangover on Monday!'

The young men laughed. Richard walked out the door. The laughter seemed to leave a nasty taste in his mouth. A nice hot bath, an early night, maybe this strange feeling would be gone by morning.

'Then, I'll go out and enjoy the rest of the weekend. Things will pick up.'

Things didn't really pick up. But Richard did a good job of pretending that they did. He behaved as normal desperately trying to bury the nagging anxiety in the pit of his stomach. It kept gnawing and gnawing at him never really going away. But as time went on Richard grew expert at ignoring it.

Leaning over the balcony of his home one summer's evening Richard was feeling particularly sour and angry. Pressures had been coming from almost every direction particularly from his mother.

'Richard, son, please settle down. Get married. Have children. Make me happy.'

Richard muttered under his breath, 'You've even gone and picked one out for me.'

'Oh Richard, but she's such a nice Jewish girl, an heiress with an interest in her father's business...'

Richard sighed, '... and she'll look like nothing!'

The sound of laughter attracted Richard's attention. He lifted his head to see his uncle striding down the street.

'What's he looking so cheerful about?' Richard

thought, 'and who is that girl with him?' Richard's thoughts must have been spoken out loud, because his mother came up from behind him to look at the girl that had attracted her blue-eyed boys attention.

'Oh, that is Sabina Oster, nice girl. Chemistry student I believe. Very intelligent.'

'Brains, and she's good looking!' Richard was smitten.

After courting her all around the nightclubs and dance halls of Bucharest, Richard and Sabina both knew they had the genuine article. They were in love.

On October, 23rd, 1935 they got married.

But even then Richard didn't settle down. The temptation to run around after other girls was still there and Richard gave in time and time again. Pleasure was there to be had. Richard would lie, cheat, and hurt others in order to enjoy whatever was around that looked fresh and interesting.

Richard's frantic lifestyle led to a life-threatening situation.

'Mr. Wurmbrand, I am afraid you have tuberculosis.'

The doctor's diagnosis brought Richard out in a sweat.

'Tuberculosis. That's extremely dangerous. Isn't it?'

'Yes, I'm afraid it is. We are going to have to discuss your treatment.'

Richard had felt ill for some time. Coughing and spluttering had become part of the daily routine.

'There's a good sanatorium in the countryside that I know of.' The Doctor rummaged around in his desk. 'Ah! Here's the address. I'll arrange for you to attend until the end of your convalescence. Good rest, good food, good air on top of excellent nursing care. We'll soon have you back on your feet.'

Richard was soon on his way to the hill country, where forests bloomed and birds sang. It was here that he rested for the first time in his life. But it was here that Richard was given time to think – it wasn't that easy facing his past.

'My mother, I treated her so badly, she wept and cried over me. I've even made my wife cry. I find it so easy to hurt people. There have been so many women that I've just used and chucked aside. Then I've talked about them afterwards. I've laughed at them with the boys at work. We've all enjoyed a good joke at the expense of the women I've hurt.'

Richard's heart felt the first pangs of guilt and the tears came. Silently at first, but soon he was bent over, praying earnestly to the God he didn't believe in.

'God, I know that you do not exist. But if perhaps you do exist, which I deny – it is up to you to show yourself to me. It is not my duty to seek you.'

Richard, the atheist[3], had prayed.

Over the next few weeks Richard's thoughts were more and more about God, about life, about what it all meant to him, Richard Wurmbrand.

When looking at his face in the mirror one morning Richard remembered something.

'I used to believe that men and women are only a collection of cells, chemicals, and bones with skin and tissue holding it all together. I used to think that when we died all that happened was that we got put in a box in the ground. We would then decompose into the dusty earth as a collection of salts and minerals. But when I think of my dead father I still think about him as my dad. I

---

3. Atheist – person who believes that there is no God.

never think about him as dead. I don't think about a pile of dust and minerals. It is my father, and I love him. When I think about him I think about his love, his laugh, his winning smile. Why is this?'

Richard's thoughts on death were often accompanied with thoughts about God. Confused, sometimes he would think about Jesus Christ. Richard was puzzled about the Son of God.

'What about that verse in the Bible when Jesus' enemies say to him, "If you are the Son of God come down from the Cross".' Just then Jesus dies. 'It looks like his enemies were right, that he was wrong. When Jesus died did he lose? Why did he die?' Richard had so many questions!

Every morning Richard's thoughts would end with, 'I wish I could have met and talked to Jesus for myself.'

As the months went on, Richard's tuberculosis started to leave him. He was getting better.

'You're not out of the woods yet, however. There is still quite a bit of recuperation to be getting on with.' The chief nurse stood stiffly beside Richard as he basked in the morning sun.

'We recommend a stay in the mountains. There are lots of villages so you can take your pick. Just tell us which one you want to go to and we'll help you to arrange transport and accommodation. This is just another step on your road to full recovery.'

Richard sat and pondered a while about which village he would most like to stay in for the next couple of months. There was one village in particular that caught his attention.

'Yes, that's the one.'

In a day or so Richard was on his way. And someone was waiting for him.

* * *

The little sunshine that Richard could see through his prison window was dimming quite quickly now – even though it was still quite early on in the evening. Richard was getting quite hungry, having not eaten anything since round about mid-day. Thinking about the miraculous healing from tuberculosis kept his spirits up.

'Yes, and the best bit of my story is still to come. I remember it as if it were just yesterday ... the little cottage, the long sofa and the carpenter – praise the Lord for the carpenter...

* * *

Round about the time Richard had prayed his first prayer – way down in the sanatorium – a long way up in the mountains an old carpenter was praying.

'My God, I have served you on earth and I wish to have my reward on earth as well as in Heaven. And my reward should be that I should not die before I bring a Jew to Christ, because Jesus was from the Jewish people. But I am poor, old and sick. I cannot go around and seek a Jew. In my village there are none. Bring Thou a Jew into my village and I will do my best to bring him to Christ.'

Imagine the old carpenter's joy when he heard that there was a Jew in his village.

'Who is this Jew? What's he doing here? Where can I find him?'

'His name is Richard Wurmbrand, he is recovering from tuberculosis and you can find him in that little

21

cottage at the end of the road. Don't you go pestering him now! Remember – he is a sick man!'

But the little carpenter made it his mission to befriend Richard and befriend him he did. Richard Wurmbrand was his answer to prayer.

'Please read this Bible for me friend.'

And Richard read it – only this time it was different. As Richard was reading it, the carpenter and his wife prayed for hours that this new friend of theirs would come to know Jesus.

And as Richard read this Bible his eyes would mist over. He could hardly make out the words as the tears poured out with every passage – each one a message straight to his heart from God. He would lie stretched out on the long sofa reading what God wanted to say to Richard Wurmbrand.

All Richard could see was Christ's purity and Richard's impurity, Christ's love and Richard's hatred, Christ's life of goodness and Richard's life of wickedness and sin. Richard now belonged to Jesus. Richard realised that Jesus had died because of him. It was Richard who should have suffered but Jesus' love was so great that he took Richard's punishment and suffering instead. Richard looked at Jesus and saw him as he really was – the winner not the loser. Richard believed. Richard was saved. Christ had been waiting for him all his life and now they met.

* * *

Praise the Lord! Richard's heart sang out over the joy of his salvation, even behind the prison bars.

'Praise the Lord. Hallelujah!'

As Richard breathed in the beautiful feeling of peace

22

and hope he realised he no longer felt any fear. In remembering how God had cared for him in the past Richard could now look to the future. He knew as well as anybody what lay ahead – imprisonment, torture, even death, yet he stared the future right in the eye and said, 'I will look at this prison as an answer to prayer. It will give new meaning to my past life. I cannot wait to discover what strange and wonderful discoveries lie in store for me.'

Half an hour had passed since he had sat down to battle with his fears and anxieties, but in a sense he had covered a whole lifetime.

'God has seen me through it all. He will do it again.'

Sabina!

Richard tried to snatch a couple of minutes sleep. Time seemed to drag on and on. He stretched out his arms as far as they would go.

'I feel so stiff... Ow! My leg hurts.' He had bruises everywhere. Richard could hardly move without feeling a twinge running up one leg or down the other. Another twinge and Richard gave up the idea of an early sleep and anyway his nose was twitching now.

'What is that disgusting smell?' Wafting up the corridor a most peculiar smell had started to annoy him. A faint aroma of sour milk on top of what could only be described as the smell of pure starch. The smell left a sickly, sticky taste at the back of your throat.

'It must be dinner,' thought Richard. And he was right. A clatter announced the arrival of Richard's first meal in captivity. The trolley squealed its way up the long corridor and a rough pair of hands shoved a metal dish in the door. Slamming the door behind him the guard then re-checked the prisoner through the spyhole.

'Enjoy!' he sniggered sarcastically. A plate of boiled barley and black mouldy bread sat there, on the floor, stodgy, cold and unappetising. No doubt the guard would be off home soon to enjoy a lovely meal prepared by his wife. Richard's thoughts meandered back to Sabina.

'... Sabina ... my lovely wife ... I am missing you so much already.'

* * *

'I don't believe it! What can you mean behaving like this! I am not going to pretend that I like this, Richard, not one bit!'

Richard had returned home from the little mountain village to share the wonderful news of his salvation with his beautiful wife. If Richard had thought she would rejoice with him over the news, he was sadly mistaken. Sabina was livid!

'What were you worried about. Why did you have to go and change things. We were fine the way we were. We're still young and with so much to enjoy in life. But no, you have to go and spoil things. I wanted to go to that new wine bar tonight but what are we going to do now – go to church?!'

'Sabina,' Richard looked longingly into the steely face of his beloved. 'I intend to be baptised – baptised as a Christian.'

Sabina's face turned to a paler shade of grey. She turned round and walked out of the room.

'My husband is joining the enemy.' That was all she could think of.

To Sabina, all Christians were against Jews. Christians were to be hated like the Nazis. Sabina's eyes darkened. Her teeth clenched, she stormed about the house.

'What does he think he is doing? How can Richard even think about becoming a Christian?'

Sabina's black mood sank so low that she even thought about killing herself. It would be better than living her life as the wife of a Christian. But Richard was patient with his young wife. He reasoned with her and gently used her natural sense of curiosity against her.

'Come and see what the inside of a church is really like Sabina, come on, just the once.'

She came.

'Look at this picture of Jesus, that's a picture of his mother there.' Richard pointed at the two pictures. Sabina looked – curiosity getting the better of her again.

'Jesus and his mother – they're Jewish!' Richard smiled. 'And look at this Bible – the Commandments here – you learnt these yourself as a child and this book here is The Psalms of David. Look Sabina, hundreds of years before Jesus came, the Jewish people in the Old Testament knew he was coming.'

Sabina remained unconvinced, and besides, there were still all these parties to be enjoyed.

'I am not going to spend my Sundays in a church. I've far better things to do! I enjoy life too much to spend it in a boring old church!'

One Sunday evening, Sabina was feeling particularly fed up.

'I want to go and see a film Richard. Come on let's skip church and go into town.'

It must have been the third or fourth time that night that Sabina had tried to persuade Richard to accompany her to the cinema. Richard decided it was time that he took another approach with his wife.

'I've tried persuading her with reason and arguments – it just hasn't worked.' Richard turned to Sabina and gave her quite a surprise.

'All right, if you want to see a film, that's what we will go and do – because I love you!' Richard put on his coat, grabbed his wallet and ushered Sabina out the door.

As they walked down the main street they discussed

what film they should go and see. Sabina could not decide so Richard put his master plan into action.

'How about this one?' Richard suggested. Sabina nodded. She was surprised.

'Yes, that one will do.'

Richard had deliberately chosen the film that looked as if it would be the most wicked and immoral film on show. Two hours later they left their seats at the cinema and went to sit in the cafe round the corner. Sabina was in the middle of enjoying a lovely cream cake when Richard decided that now was the time. What he said made Sabina almost drop the cream cake in her lap.

'Sabina, you're no fun any more, you should go home now, I am going to go out and find a young girl – maybe go dancing and then I'll take her back to an hotel for the evening.'

Coughing and spluttering Sabina turned on Richard.

'What did you say?'

'But you wanted me to come out with you tonight. You saw what the hero got up to in the film. Why should I not go and do the same? Every man becomes what he looks at, and if you want me to look at films like that then you will just have to put up with a rotten husband! On the other hand if you would like to have a good husband then let me go to church – and come with me sometimes.'

'All right. I'll agree with you about the film, it was disgusting. And there is no way I'm going to put up with a husband like that!' Sabina stood up, left what remained of her cream cake and announced, 'I'm ready to go home now Richard, it's quite late.'

Some time later Richard set the next stage of his plan

27

into action. He knew he was on the right track. Richard mentioned that perhaps they should go to a party that night. Sabina was overjoyed.

'I'll just go and get changed. Oh. What will I wear?' Sabina charged around her wardrobe choosing one thing and discarding the next. When they were both ready they set off to the friend's apartment.

Sabina coughed as she walked through the door.

'My word, this place is thick with smoke.' She looked around the room at the crowd of puffing cigarettes. Every corner had somebody flat on the floor, already too stupid with drink to even stand up.

Sabina wasn't too sure about this party now.

'What do these people think they are doing?' Sabina exclaimed as more than one couple started kissing openly in the middle of the room.

'Let's go home Richard,' she whispered. 'If we slip away now nobody will even notice.'

Richard said something which was rather surprising.

'Why leave? The party's only just started.'

As the evening wore on the drinking got more and more out of control. The couples in the middle of the room became more and more obvious. They didn't seem to care who saw them. Sabina's cheeks flushed with the embarrassment of the situation.

'Richard, can't we leave now? It's past midnight.'

Richard didn't seem to care.

'Sabina, its far too early. The night is young!'

At 1.00 am. Sabina tried again. Richard wouldn't move. At 1.30 am. Richard still hadn't changed his mind. But at just after 2.00 am. Richard realised that Sabina was thoroughly sickened of parties. The whole sordid occasion had made her feel quite sick.

The young couple stepped out of the smoke-filled apartment, out into the clean fresh air of the early morning.

Sabina held Richard's hand and smiled.

'I am going straight to your pastor's house to ask him to baptise me as a Christian. It will be like taking a bath after all that filth.'

Richard's head fell back and he laughed out loud.

'Sabina – you have waited so long. Surely you can wait until the morning. Let the poor pastor have his sleep!'

Hand in hand the young couple walked home, together.

Richard's Guest

'Thank you, Lord, that you are with Sabina now. You will look after her. I know she couldn't be in better hands.' Richard sat, legs crossed, on the floor of the cell, chewing his nails, trying to save his last bit of black bread for later on.

'Who knows when I will get anything else to eat?'

Richard was still really hungry.

Standing up to his full height Richard looked out the little window. A gate had clanged shut and voices could be heard in the courtyard outside.

Curiosity got the better of him and he scanned the courtyard below for any signs of life.

Richard just made out the sounds of muffled footsteps and the familiar swish of long priestly robes. The figure of a local priest emerged in the middle of the courtyard. The priest marched alongside a prison officer. The whole situation made Richard think.

'He seems on quite friendly terms with this guard. They are chatting together as they cross the courtyard. Maybe friendly is not the right word. The priest does seem a bit tense. But he's not in chains so he's not a prisoner. There's no bag over his head. No rough treatment. Yes, there is something strange going on here.'

As Richard looked at the Priest he noticed how he looked one way then the other. The Priest did not want to be seen. That could only mean one thing.

'He is an informer.'

Richard had heard many times about priests who, under pressure from the Communist government, would betray people in their congregations. A young man would go to his minister with a problem, the minister would listen to the young man's anguish, give him advice as to how he should deal with his sins and then pass on the information to the Secret Police. The young man would be in jail before he could blink. One more prisoner and one more cell full to overflowing.

Richard's thoughts went back to his own situation.

'They will start questioning me soon. They will keep at me and at me until they break me.' Richard bowed his head in silent, urgent prayer.

'Lord please protect my friends and family. They need protection from me, Lord. How will I control my tongue under interrogation? When the torture comes will I be able to hide what I really know? Lord, perhaps you could stop my tongue, perhaps you could make me forget?'

Then a sudden thought, straight from heaven, flashed into his mind.

'Of course, I remember now!' Leaning back against the concrete wall Richard thanked God.

'Thank you, Lord, that you have written, "*Don't be afraid*" 366 times in your word. One for every day of the year. It is amazing that it is not just 365 times – that would mean you had forgotten all about February the 29th. And that's today! The day of my arrest. The day of my imprisonment. You have not forgotten! And I will not be afraid. Hallelujah!

* * *

Time went on and on. Richard had no way of telling what hour had passed and what hour was still to come. He had a rough idea by the fact that he had already eaten most of his cold supper that it must be coming on for about 9 or 10 o'clock.

Still no interrogators came.

Richard returned to his own thoughts again.

'I must remember everything that I have learned. I have read and heard about so many different Christians who suffered and died for our Lord. I am not the first to suffer, I must remember that. I must prepare myself as well as possible.'

Richard knew that the Communists would do everything they could to trip him up.

'They will even try and persuade me that as a Christian pastor I should always tell the truth. But I know that cannot always be the case. If I tell the truth to the Communists others will join me here in prison. I will not be responsible for bringing someone else to torture. I will do my level best to totally confuse those interrogators. They are the enemy – God's enemy. They won't know if they're coming or going. I will tell them to go left when they should be going right!'

* * *

The following morning Richard woke up with a start. The loud noise coming from the other end of the corridor was just the authorities way of waking them up, but Richard was glad he was awake, he had a plan to put into action.

'Sabina must know where I am. If the others know what's happened to me then they will be careful. I may not have been the only one spied on.'

There was a way to get a message out but it meant asking one of the guards for help.

'Well I'll have to take the risk. It's now or never.'

A pair of knobbly wrinkled hands dropped a plate of lumpy sludge on the floor of his cell. Breakfast was here. Richard sprang into action.

'I must get a message to my wife. We have money. She will pay you.'

The guard looked around anxiously. There was no one about. He looked into Richard's deep blue eyes and nodded.

Over the next few weeks Sabina exchanged messages with Richard. The guard received £500 for being the courier. Richard wrote Sabina a letter on the back of a chocolate wrapper:

'*My dearest wife, I thank you for your sweetness. I'm well. Richard.*'

The money stopped when the Communists decided to take everything the Wurmbrands had, even their flat. But the guard had struck up a friendship with Richard, the crazy pastor who wrote love letters to his wife on the back of chocolate wrappers. One morning the guard passed on a very important piece of information.

Richard was feeling just a little stiff in the back that morning so he got up and started doing what little exercise he could. First Richard raised one arm up in the air then the other, followed by a brisk jog around his cramped living quarters. As his tall athletic body pounded around the four walls of the prison cell the guard stopped at the spy hole, looking one way and then the other to check that no one could see him. Richard noticed his long knobbly finger beckoning to him through the spyhole.

'Ah, what news this morning, friend?'

'Only that the Swedish ambassador has been asking after you. The authorities, however, are still adamant that you are no longer in the country. The latest story is that you have ran away with the mission funds to Denmark!'

Richard thanked the guard and continued with his jog. What did it matter what these people said and did? The Lord knew who he was and where he was.

'He is in control, nobody else!'

* * *

Richard stared out the window again. It was good to look at something different than the concrete walls. As he counted the days he couldn't believe it had only been 3 or 4 since he had been dragged off the city streets and thrown into this little cell. There had been no interrogations, some threats, a little bullying, but no torture. Richard's nerves were on edge with all the waiting.

As he sat down to wait for the next plate of boiled barley, some noises at the other end of the corridor made him sit up straight and pay attention. Footsteps marched down the corridor and stopped short at the door to his cell.

'What's going on? Why, they're coming in here. Is this it? Is this going to be the interrogation?'

The door opened wide and instead of a collection of rough guards charging into his cell a well-dressed government official stood in the doorway.

Richard couldn't believe his eyes. It was Comrade Patrascanu, the Minister of Justice.

'Amazing. I used to see his face almost every day in the newspapers – and here he is standing in my cell! If he is going to interrogate me then they must think I have something worth knowing!'

But after a millisecond of thought Richard realised something was not quite right.

The man wore an exclusive suit, a well-pressed shirt, his hair was slicked back in the latest style, but where was his tie? Richard looked down at the man's highly polished leather shoes and it suddenly dawned on him what was wrong. The man had no shoelaces. Instead of interrogation this man was here as a prisoner.

The door closed. The key turned and all of a sudden Richard had a new cell mate.

Lying back on his bench Richard stared at the well-dressed, very confident prisoner.

'Well I never! Whatever next?' Richard thought.

* * *

Comrade Patrascanu had actually been one of the men who started Communism in Romania.

Communism was a name given to a certain type of government. If you were a Communist you believed in Communism. Richard knew how Communists, like Patrascanu, ruled Romania. Communists didn't want anything to do with God so nobody in Romania was allowed to worship him. Communists didn't like anyone who did not do things the way they wanted. If you disobeyed them you were put in prison. Richard, however, felt it was more important to obey God. So he did and Richard, as a result, was now serving a prison sentence.

The Minister of Justice smiled thinly at Richard and sat himself down on the other bench. Swinging his legs up he made himself comfortable. The former government official was obviously weighing up the situation. Patrascanu then shrugged his shoulders and looked across the cell to where Richard sat, quietly whistling an old hymn tune.

'Well,' Patrascanu took a deep breath, 'this is not my first time in prison, I'll cope, but boy, this place is cold!'

This light-hearted remark broke the ice between them and Richard realised that despite what this man had done in the past he was actually quite a likeable fellow.

The two prisoners shared stories together, comparing how each had arrived in the Calea Rahova jail. Patrascanu's story was a sorry one. Though a powerful, rich and prominent person in Romanian society he had been rejected as a traitor by the very people who had worked alongside him. They had supported him and Patrascanu thought they had respected him. But their hunger for more power claimed him as just another victim.

'The main culprits are Techari Georgescu, Vasile Luia – you'll know him, he's the Minister of Finance, and then there is the Foreign Minister, Ana Pauker. They all ganged up against me some time ago. It was only today that I gave them their final piece of ammunition. I asked someone if all the rumours about prisoners being tortured were true. I was told, "Of course they are. These people withhold information from the state. They don't deserve any pity." This deeply disturbed me so I made an official protest. Next thing I know my chauffeur is off sick, I get in the car as usual and two Secret Police officers get in after me. So here I am!'

Richard wondered how he should discuss religion with this ardent Communist, but just as he was going over the question in his mind the door opened and a guard came in with Richard's meal. Boiled barley, dry bread.

'Nothing new here,' said Richard.

But then Patrascanu's meal came in, served on a beautifully set-out tray complete with cutlery, glassware and a linen napkin. Richard sneaked a look at what they served a Government official.

Grilled chicken on a bed of fresh vegetables, new potatoes with melted butter, delicious portions of fresh fruit, all washed down with a cool bottle of sparkling white wine. Richard's nose twitched. His mouth was watering so much Richard was sure Patrascanu would see him licking his lips if he wasn't careful. Richard battled to keep his stomach under control, but he couldn't. His belly growled.

Richard's new friend took a glass of wine and without a word pushed the tray over to Richard. Richard stared.

'Food. Real Food.' It was all Richard could think about. Bowing his head he thanked the Lord. Patrascanu looked on bemused. Just to remind Richard where the food had come from Patrascanu coughed, 'Eat up friend, enjoy it. I have no appetite myself.'

Richard lifted the fork then the knife and tucked in. He didn't stop until every last bite was gone – licked, savoured, chewed and swallowed.

That night Richard lay back and thanked the Lord for the food.

'It's just so good to go to sleep on a full stomach.'

With that Richard closed his eyes and nodded off.

Richard eventually managed to get his new cellmate to talk to him about God. In fact Patrascanu talked to Richard in a way he could not talk to any other person. Richard was in jail with very little chance of ever getting out. Richard wasn't going to tell anybody about anything.

Looking across at the dishevelled pastor, he told Richard about why he had first joined the Communist party.

'You see, my father made life very difficult for us by supporting the Germans in the First World War. When the allies won we were cut off from everybody, totally disgraced and I even had to go to Germany to get an education.'

'Why Communism then?' Richard asked.

'After coming back from Germany the Communists were the only people who wanted me!'

Patrascanu was bitter. He was carrying around a huge grudge against the world and particularly against Christianity.

'There's one thing I want to know Wurmbrand.'

Richard looked across at the hot angry face of the ex-Minister of Justice.

'Why do you insist on belonging to such hypocrisy? Look at this church of yours. More crime comes from the church than from criminals. The whole organisation is riddled with mistakes and errors. You can't be serious about it?'

Richard took his time in replying.

'My friend, you must look at the results. There has been a lot of sadness which has stained the church over the years. But it has also poured out love and care all over the world.'

Richard smiled. Patrascanu grimaced.

'... Best of all, we have Christ as our leader. He is pure and good, the holiest of all. Now let's compare this with Communism.'

Patrascanu squirmed. Richard was going to give it to him full blast.

'Marx, the first Communist, was a drunkard. Lenin's wife admits he was a gambler and as for Stalin, even though he said, "We must care for men like flowers", he killed his own wife. Communism has wiped out millions of innocent victims, bankrupted countries and now everywhere in Romania we live in hate and fear. Show me the good side in that!'

Patrascanu withdrew, sulking. Warming to his topic Richard continued.

'Mr Patrascanu. You have used people and then cast them aside. Now it is your turn. Your friends have used you and thrown you away like worthless rubbish.'

Patrascanu turned to Richard and cursed.

'They will follow me!' he said. 'Those so-called friends – they will follow me! They will either be shot or imprisoned. Not one of them will escape.'

Not one of them did.

Questions, Questions!

'Uh, what's that?' Patrascanu mumbled in his sleep. His dreams were not pleasant. Faces of people he had cheated, robbed, imprisoned, chased him up this corridor then another. His cramped body moved from one uncomfortable position to another. Richard yawned and looked over at his troubled companion.

'I often lie awake when others sleep, or try to sleep. An aura of peace envelops this room on occasions such as this. This is a time to meet with God quietly and alone. I relish the rest, the sense of security even behind these iron bars.' Richard muttered to himself quietly. The sound of his own voice was just something different to listen to as the evening drew to a close.

'It must be just after 10 pm.' Richard thought to himself. Although there was no clock anywhere to be seen Richard could make rough judgements of time thanks to the window – his one vantage point on the outside world. He curled up with his thoughts for company.

'Silence covers the prison as a blanket covers a sleeping child. Occasionally the blanket falls off and you hear a prisoner's nightmare screams. Sometimes I hear faint snores from the next cell. I remember Mihai sleeping underneath his covers. Sabina would take him through and tuck him in warm and snug. Then she would get up in the middle of the night sometimes to find he'd thrown them all off in his sleep.' Richard's thoughts rambled on and on. 'Perhaps even now Sabina is checking on Mihai, picking up the covers from the floor and wrapping them round him again. It's as if I can see them there. Mihai's face calm, peaceful, Sabina's eyes tired but loving.

Richard sat up and called out of the window. 'Sabina, I love you.'

His heartfelt cry seemed to take the chill off the prison walls. He lay down again on his mattress, smiling, and letting his eyes wander round the prison cell, picking out familiar objects here and there.

There was the dim outline of the cell door with the spyhole, the bucket conveniently placed in the corner, and the gentle snores from the cell down the corridor. Everything was just as it always was.

A brilliant white star shone piercingly into the dark cell. It was like a beam of hope as Richard lay there basking in the quietness.

'In your presence there is fullness of joy....' Richard's quick prayer of thanks was interrupted by the sharp ringing sound of a slamming door.

The light was switched on. Richard was ordered sharply to get dressed. Patrascanu peered out from behind the covers.

'Quickly now,' the guard snapped.

'Pst ...,' Patrascanu bent over towards Richard. 'Put on that old coat of yours. If they start punching you it will give more protection.'

'Not much,' thought Richard as they pulled a pair of goggles over his eyes.

The march down the corridor was brisk and noisy as usual. Every action taken within the prison walls was meant to frighten and intimidate the prison population.

The march over, Richard found himself seated on a chair, and looking up his eyes stared straight into a bright white light shining straight into his face. He winced trying to see beyond the light. Was there anybody there?

A voice spoke up.

'Prisoner!'

The voice came closer.

'You will tell us everything.'

The voice came closer.

'Everything, do you hear?'

The voice came up to his ear.

'In that desk there is paper and a pen – write it all out!'

Richard looked puzzled.

'Everything, every detail, you know what we need to know. Don't hold anything back!'

Reaching out Richard opened the drawer and took out the paper and pen.

Fumbling with the pen, Richard wondered who would read this.

'Party officials possibly ... unbelievers most of them ... what a chance to share the Lord with people who desperately need him! It is an opportunity sent from God!!'

Richard's fingers itched to get started and his pen flew across the pages. A whole hour passed. The interrogator was beginning to yawn, Richard was getting into his stride.

The paper and pen were removed – the transcript placed inside an official looking briefcase. Goggles on again, Richard was led back to his cell. He lay back exhausted. Tonight was only the beginning. What might come next – he didn't know. Patrascanu's heavy snoring reverberated around the four walls.

'At least somebody seems to be having a good night's sleep,' thought Richard.

* * *

11.00 am., two days later. Richard is interrogated. Paper, pens, questions, writing. Shouts, answers, more questions.

2.30 am. the next night. Richard is interrogated. Orders, shouts, questions, writings. Shouts, answers, more questions.

3.30 pm. in the afternoon. Richard is interrogated once more. Writing, writing, more writing. Questions upon questions. No answer seems good enough. No answer is long enough. Interrogation. Interrogation. Interrogation. Endless interrogation.

No time is the wrong time.

Any time is the right time.

* * *

'I'm exhausted.' Richard heaved a sigh as he flopped down on to his mattress. The interrogations were sprung on him morning, noon and night. Every day for a week, then he might not see or hear anything for another week. The schedule, if you could call it that, was gruelling, mentally exhausting and emotionally charged. Patrascanu looked across the room at Richard. Richard was praying. Silently his lips moved, his heart opened, and he relaxed. Patrascanu coughed politely. Richard smiled and looked up.

'Yes friend, how can I help?'

Shuffling his feet Patrascanu muttered, 'I used to pray, but I gave it up.'

Surprised and quite intrigued Richard asked him why.

'Your Jesus asks too much. Especially when you are young.'

Very softly Richard shook his head.

'I've never thought of it like that. In fact, I think of it like this...' Richard paused to gather his thoughts. 'I've told you about little Mihai?'

Patrascanu smiled.

'Yes Wurmbrand, many, many times.'

'Well, Mihai is quite small but he likes to buy his papa a birthday present. One year it was a book of poems, another year he bought me a pocket knife. He likes to buy something that I will enjoy. Mihai's eyes will light up when I open the parcel revealing his present inside. But the little fellow never has any money of his own to buy me presents. So every birthday he comes to me and asks for money and he goes with his mother to chose some little thing for his papa.'

The simple homely warmth of the story brought a warm glow to Patrascanu's heart.

'When Jesus asks us for faith, for strength, for commitment to him, if we ask him for these he will give them to us. So what he asks us for he will give us and we become better people as a result.'

Patrascanu smiled, but said nothing. The next morning a guard came and took Patrascanu away.

'Comrade Patrascanu is leaving for another prison.'

Richard would never see him again.

* * *

Richard stared at the empty mattress.

'Alone again...,' Richard muttered, '... but not really...' Richard smiled as he turned again to prayer.

Death and Depression

On his own again there was no one to advise Richard to put his overcoat on when the interrogators came to call.

Richard missed Patrascanu but was given precious little time to mope as the inquisitor Vasilu took over the Wurmbrand case.

With beady little eyes and the strange habit of speaking out of the corner of his mouth Vasilu was out to get Richard.

Vasilu's sweaty palms held a list of questions, typed on white government paper, with an official stamp in the corner.

Richard held his pen tightly.

'What now?' he wondered.

'The first question is ...,' the beady eyes looked up, 'Who do you know?'

Richard fumbled with his pen.

'Don't think about it!' Vasilu snapped. 'Just do it! Everyone you know, where you met them, what you have done together, your relationships, how long you have known them, what they do – everything!'

Richard hesitated. He was not going to betray his friends. What should he do?

Vasilu turned quickly and yelled in Richard's ear. 'Don't pick and choose – Write! Write! Do it now!!'

Richard drummed his fingers on the wooden desk, then made a start.

His thoughts came quick and fast.

'There are people that the Secret Police already know I have had contact with – the church members, my assistants. I can't protect them – only the Lord can do that.'

Richard wrote them down.

'I know some Communist members of parliament. I will put them in my list. It might help me – who knows?'

Richard wrote them down.

'Ah! ... informers ... I'll write down their names. I know a few of them.'

Richard wrote them down.

'Well that's over two pages worth of people ... not bad. The Secret Police either have files on them already or have already persuaded them to change sides.'

Vasilu reached over and snatched the piece of paper away.

'Question number two is – What have you done against the state? Give me a list of all your crimes against Communism.'

'What am I accused of?' Richard asked.

A podgy, white fist came down on the table with a thud!

'You know what you have done! Get it off your chest! Write, write and keep writing.'

Richard took up the pen once more and started to write. Vasilu went out the door for a smoke, leaving his young deputy in charge of the prisoner. Richard continued to write. After a few minutes he felt a hand on his shoulder. Startled he turned round – one young deputy stood there, an edge of fear surrounding him.

'I have some information I think you should know.' Reaching down to his briefcase he pulled out a thick brown file, laid it on the desk in front of Richard and opened it. Inside were one or two transcripts of interviews and interrogations, statements and quotes and other official-looking documents. The young deputy brought some to Richard's particular attention. They were statements written against him by men he had trusted, friends and neighbours, who had turned against him.

A door slammed halfway up the corridor. The thick brown folder vanished back into its briefcase. Everything went on as before.

Incarcerated again in his prison cell Richard thought about the statements in the brown file.

'These signatures must have been forced out of them.'

Richard shivered at the thought.

* * *

Long, empty days passed slowly between frenzied interrogations. Richard used the free time wisely to prepare for the next onslaught of twenty questions.

One morning the prison authorities authorised a barber to give the inmates a short back and sides. A regulation removal of all hair on the head and face. The barber's razor skimmed across Richard's chin, deftly lifting off the ragged stubble. Richard sat as still as possible quite enjoying the break in routine. The barber leaned over to take a closer look at his client – checking to see that no one was taking any notice of them – the barber whispered, 'Sabina is well and is carrying on your work.'

Richard made do with whispering, 'Hallelujah!'

His wife was well, Mihai was being looked after. God was looking after all of them.

However, as the days passed, Richard was continually under an attack of a different kind altogether. A dark period of depression set in as Richard thought long and hard about what might lie ahead.

'Torture lies ahead ... no way to turn ... it's just there ... in my future ... not long now. What will I do? Oh God no! What will I do? Please help me!'

Richard's throat was blocked with emotion. Anxiety weighed down upon him almost smothering him.

'What will it be like to die? I know I will go straight to Christ, but the pain and torture, I can't bear to think about it. Oh Lord, I don't know how I'll stop myself from giving in. I know so much and I could hurt so many people. Will I just cave in under the torture and tell them what they want? Please God, stop me.'

His hands shook, the cold sweat oozed out of his palms, he rubbed them dry on his overcoat, and paced the cell this way and that. Wrapping his arms around himself to keep them from shaking he looked desperately for some way out.

'Escape? Impossible. The only way I'll get out of this prison is if I am dead and placed in a wooden box!'

Richard stopped.

'What?'

His heart beat faster.

'No!?'

But that was the answer. Richard's mind was set.

'I will kill myself. Yes I will. I am a Christian, I will go straight to be with Jesus. If I am dead I can't hurt anyone. It will be worth it!"

The cold thought behan to take hold. Richard put the

plan into action. The next time the prison doctor did his rounds, Richard had a speech already set out.

'Sir, can you help me?'

'What is it? I haven't got all day.'

'Lately I haven't been able to sleep. It's been 3 weeks since I had a decent sleep ... and it is not helping in the interrogations. You see I can't remember all the answers the interrogators need. Do you have anything that could help me?'

The doctor walked straight into Richard's trap and prescribed a sleeping pill to be taken every night under supervision of a guard. Every night the guard would come in with the sleeping pill.

'Prisoner, open up.'

The pill was placed on Richard's tongue. Quickly Richard hid it under his tongue and pretended to swallow. He then opened up his mouth for inspection. The guard, not seeing any pill, left the prisoner behind – who promptly spat the pill out and hid it. The hoard of pills increased steadily – each one hidden carefully in Patrascanu's old mattress.

Sometimes the fear of torture would get too much for Richard. He would then think about his store of sleeping pills and breathe easier. They were his escape, his last resort, his final option.

But sometimes he felt differently. One morning summer finally arrived.

'Thank God.' Richard smiled, but then he caught a glimpse of the mattress. His dark secret and black depression took hold.

'Why God, Why? There's a girl singing outside. I can hear a tram in the distance taking people to work. Its grinding as it goes round the corner into the next street. A mother is calling her children inside, "Silviu, Emil, Matei!" Ah, look at that beautiful flower petal – it has just floated in through the window and landed at my feet. It's so soft, so gentle. What are you doing God? I'm being forced to put an end to a life that I've dedicated to you.' At night Richard would stare into the pitch-dark sky. 'The first star is just appearing. It's so beautiful Father, so full of promise. You made this light, you sent its beam into my prison cell over millions of miles, just to console me. What am I supposed to do? What is your will Lord? I don't know. Won't you tell me? Please ... I don't want to die ... what can I do?'

The whispered prayer was heard. The prisoner woke up the next morning as a rather flustered guard bustled into his cell and bustled out again – as he went out he took the extra mattress with him.

'Right, no need for you to have two mattresses – we've been spoiling you – far too much luxury ...', the guard grunted as he pushed and shoved the mattress out the door.' With that Richard's pills vanished.

'Oh no,' thought Richard. Then he chuckled. The more he thought about it the funnier it got. Richard's head bent back and he laughed out loud.

'God doesn't want my suicide. He wants me alive, whatever's ahead, whatever he has planned, whatever the suffering, God will provide the strength! I'll get through it *whatever* it is.'

The '*whatever*' wasn't very far away.

Torture

'You have been playing with us.' Colonel Dulgheru, lay back in his chair, his pale lily-white hands silently stroking the leather arm. 'You have had it too easy up to now, but things are going to change for you! Yes indeed...'

The menace in his voice, the edge that gave his breath that sharp death-like quality, sent shivers down your spine. Richard sat and shivered.

'Prisoner, it is time for results! Results that I have waited for, for a long time.' Dulgheru paused again. His eyes left his lily-white hands for a second and cut straight into Richard. Breathing slow and steady, Dulgheru's eyes returned to his hands. One hand moved smoothly and silently over the other as if in a perpetual cleansing ritual. An astute and hardened Communist, Dulgheru's reputation cut a lot of ice in the prison cell. He was the boss. He got results. The grand inquisitor was never a failure.

'You have been playing with us. Yes indeed ... and we are tired of this game!'

Questions flashed from Dulgheru's mouth like bullets out of a six-shooter. Persistent and to the point Dulgheru surrounded Richard on all sides with a question here or an order there. Richard realised that every word he spoke would have to be chosen with the utmost care.

'Every word, Every word.' Richard willed his tongue into submission. 'Stay in control Richard. Be careful!'

Dulgheru's questions continued relentlessly, one after the other, after the other. Like a hound on the scent Dulgheru thought he could smell something somewhere. He was on the chase. Richard Wurmbrand was his quarry and Richard Wurmbrand had no place to hide.

Weeks followed weeks and Richard underwent a programme designed for the specific destruction of all strength of mind, body and will.

After being pushed back into his cell one evening, Richard looked for his bed. It was no longer there. Just a rickety old chair in the corner. Sitting down he attempted sleep. Shifting from one uncomfortable spot to another Richard fought hard to keep his balance on the chair and sleep at the same time. It was either the chair or the stone cold floor. Not much of a choice. Just as Richard's eyes finally relaxed in sleep the spyhole rattled. Richard jumped up.

'Are they coming for me again? No, it was just the guard checking. Back to sleep now. I'm just so tired.'

Richard's eyes closed again.

Two minutes later...

Clank. Clank. The spy hole opened up again and again it slammed shut.

'The guards are busy tonight!'

Richard shifted, trying to get to sleep again.

Two minutes later...

Clank. Clank. Another pair of eyes scans the room.

Sleep eludes Richard once more. Every time sleep appears round the corner another pair of eyes appear at the spyhole – and every two minutes throughout the night. From dusk to dawn the guards never leave him alone.

Clank. Clank. Another pair of eyes scrutinises the prisoner.

Clank. Clank . Richard is shouted at to stay awake.

Clank. Clank. Richard is kicked in the stomach after falling asleep.

Clank. Clank. Richard wakes up again for the twentieth time that night.

Richard dozed for minutes here and there but the prison authorities began to hatch a master plan that kept him well and truly awake.

Richard wandered in the land of dreams – a fantasy freedom behind bars.

'What is that noise? Am I hearing music? What a lovely dream this is.'

But it is no dream.

Beautiful soft music wafted through his cell. Richard woke slowly, confused, tired.

'What's my prison door doing open like that?' Richard wondered. 'Where is that music coming from? Am I hearing things?' As Richard's eyes opened wider his thoughts began to clear. The music suddenly changed, becoming more sinister, distorted. A woman's voice cut through the air sobbing, screaming.

'No, no, please no. Don't, no don't, no, no!' The screams mounted higher, then higher. Richard jumped, panic-stricken, to his feet.

'Sabina! No, not Sabina!'

A whip came down, crack. Richard heard the sound of tearing flesh.

'No! No! Let her go. Don't hurt her. Leave her alone! Leave my wife alone!'

The screams crescendo to an appalling pitch. Slowly

the voice diminishes to a faint moaning, a pathetic whimper. No longer is it the voice of Sabina. This voice is a strangers voice ... another woman has been tortured ... not Sabina....

'Not my Sabina.'

Then silence. The whole prison is racked in pain. Every man's wife, sweetheart, daughter had been the victim, the tortured, the violent screamer. All had woken up to the pain of a loved one's torture.

'No, not my darling. Leave her alone.'

'My wife, they have my wife!'

'Lisa – my little girl. They're killing my little girl.'

The shouts had come from every prison cell. Mass torture through a taperecorder and a few well placed microphones.

There is a whirr, whirr, whirr of the tape running to the end then the sudden click and silence as the recorder shuts down. Sobbing, Richard slumps on to the cold stone floor, shaking, exhausted, drenched with sweat. He sleeps, but only for a minute, as clank, clank – the spyhole opens up again and another pair of eyes peers in.

* * *

The scientific name for it all was sleep deprivation. Clinical minds, doctors, psychologists all recognised its dreadful side-effects. When a mind is refused shutdown, there is great physical and mental pain as the body is urged to keep going and going and going.

Another night, another sleepless night, and Richard sat slumped over his chair.

'Oh sleep, sleep, just give me a little sleep.'

Clank, clank went the spy hole.

'The eyes, the eyes, the endless pairs of eyes.' Richard looked up through his own blood-shot pair.

Dulgheru stood in front of him as if in a nightmare.

'Do you know that I can order your execution now, tonight?'

Dulgheru's similarity to a venom-spitting snake could not be missed. His tongue dripped poison. He was deadly.

Dalgheru was so proud of himself he also strongly resembled a peacock. He strutted round Richard's cell going on and on about how Communism was the best, the only way. Anyone who was not a Communist was evil. A strange distorted opinion but one Dulgheru totally believed in. Even in rage Dulgheru epitomised the quality of self control. Even when his voice roared, or his temper flared the control was there, the ice that wouldn't melt. Richard stared eyeball to eyeball with a glacier.

'You could be dead and buried tomorrow. Nobody will think twice when I say "kill him". You'll be dead.'

Richard turned his head towards the grand inquisitor. This was another moment when Richard was given the choice to speak up or shut up. Richard did what he did best.

'Colonel, here you have the opportunity for an experiment. You say you can have me shot. I know you can. So put your hand here on my heart. If it beats rapidly, showing you that I am afraid, then know this – there is no God and therefore no eternal life. But, if it beats calmly, as if to say, "I go to the One I love", then you must think again. There is a God, and an eternal life!'

Dulgheru's veins stuck out on the side of his neck. The ice melted. The self-control vanished, momentarily, as he struck Richard full across the face. His face flushed,

Dulgheru breathed rapidly, he had lost his self-control, he had lost. He had lost to Richard, to his own emotions. Dulgheru had lost to the God he had the audacity to totally ignore.

'You are a fool,' he muttered as he left the cell. 'Tomorrow you will meet Comrade Brinzaru.'

Richard sat curled up in a dark little corner. His eyes, deep pools of blue, gazed calmly out the window.

'Brinzaru. I knew I would meet him sometime. I will not be afraid, though I walk through the valley of the Shadow, you are with me, O God. Even though I walk through Brinzaru's cave, you are with me, O God.'

Brinzaru's cave was where he kept all manner of torturous equipment such as truncheons, whips and clubs. His hairy arms, like a gorilla's, grasped each item with brute strength. These items would then be brought brutally down on bare backs, thighs, shoulders, feet.

Richard was going to meet him.

The prospect of this introduction sent a chill through Richard's blood.

'The man has no heart, that's for sure. How could he have killed that young man?'

Richard's mind wandered back. 'Last week when I was cleaning out the toilets, those soldiers were talking about him.' Richard remembered he had been scrubbing the tiles when he heard the guards muttering to each other... 'You see Brinzaru worked for a prominent politician – before the war it was. I can't remember who the man was exactly, but he had a young son. The man was quite prosperous and Brinzaru was treated as one of the family. The little child would come to him and play games with him, "Brinzaru catch this, Brinzaru lift me up, Brinzaru, Brinzaru." The boy loved him.' The guard had then flicked his cigarette ash on the clean toilet floor.

'Oh, bother, I will have to clean that up,' thought Richard as be carried on listening to the conversation.

'After the war Brinzaru rapidly rose up in the ranks of the Secret Police.'

'He must have been very popular with someone.'

'Yeah, he knew all the right people that's for sure. Anyway, one day a young man was brought into the interrogation room. Brinzaru looked up and saw the face of the young child he had sat on his knee, the little boy who had played games with him, who had sang to him. The politician's son.'

'What did he do? Was the young boy a prisoner?'

'Yes. The young man had tried to start a political movement of his own, in opposition to the government. He had been caught and imprisoned and brought to Brinzaru. Brinzaru turned to the young man and smiled, "When you were a child I used to hold you on my knee." The young man was then beaten, whipped, tortured, and finally executed by Brinzaru's own hands.'

The other guard let out a low whistle. 'What a guy! I'm glad he's not my enemy!'

This was the man that Richard was about to meet.

Richard's first meeting with Brinzaru was short, and to the point.

'Come this way,' invited Brinzaru. Richard was ushered into the chamber.

Brinzaru tenderly lifted down one torture implement after the other, displayed it to the prisoner and then gently replaced it on the shelf. It felt like he was being shown goods by some merchant or other. Brinzaru would smile menacingly with every whip or club he cradled.

Richard was admitted back into his cell alone with his thoughts. Surprisingly enough Richard would never get Brinzaru's promised beating. That night when Brinzaru inspected the cells he eventually came to Richard's.

'Still there, Christian? What's Jesus doing tonight?'

Smiling gently, Richard replied, 'He's praying for you.'

Brinzaru walked away, silent.

The beating was forgotten but torture was not. The Communists had many different methods of inflicting pain and psychological injury. The following morning Brinzaru was back.

'Stand straight facing the wall. Raise your hands above your head. Keep them there.'

Richard's torture had begun.

For hours Richard stood in the one position. His arms lost all feeling, his legs began to tremble. Soon his ankles began to swell, the fluid built up in his legs and they puffed up. Eventually Richard collapsed on the floor. His body just gave up though his mind was shouting at him to keep going. A guard rushed in and gave him a sip of water and a small crust of bread. Richard gulped them down.

'More water, please, more water.' But there was none. Richard was made to stand again. A few hours passed and one guard would leave to be replaced by another. The prisoner wasn't replaced. There was no change-over for Richard. He had to keep standing, staring, straight and still with only one wall to look at.

The guards would sometimes get bored of looking at Richard, standing, staring at the wall. To amuse themselves a little they would force him to stand in ridiculous positions, legs one way, arms another.

'Put that arm there, that's right, this hand just there, Ha ha! What a laugh. Yes and put that leg there. Now stay.'

The guard would turn away giggling to himself, and Richard would be left to suffer the pain and indignity of it all.

At all times and in all positions Richard stared at the wall. Not a second went by when his eyes weren't in contact with the grey stone slabs, the mind-numbing sameness of the square bricks piled upon square bricks.

As Richard pondered the boring old wall it was as if his mind tripped over a little thought about walls.

'Walls are referred to rather a lot in the Bible! God says in Isaiah that Israel's wrongdoings put a wall between them so sin is like a wall that stops me being with God. "With my Lord, I jump over the wall." How do I jump this wall? I can't jump this concrete wall but I can escape this torture and leap into the arms of my loving God. They can't get me there. What else is there, aah? Yes, I know, the Jewish spies came back from Jericho. "The cities are great and walled." But the walls of Jericho came crashing down. My wall can come down too at God's command. No puny little wall is going to stop him!'

Richard thought about the strong walls that surrounded big cities and the great walls that surrounded kings and queens. Walls could protect but God was the protector. But there were times when the pain just got too much. Even then Richard's thoughts about walls helped him through.

'My love is like a roe or a young hart; behold, he

standeth behind our wall.' Richard muttered the Bible verse over and over to himself. There was comfort, peace, relief just in these few words.

'I will picture my love, my Lord, just behind my wall. He is there giving me strength from behind the wall. Perhaps even in my suffering I am helping the people of God towards victory. It would be just like Moses on the mountain-top. As long as he held up his hands the people went forward victorious. I am standing here forcing my hands to stay up ... God gives us the Victory.'

All of a sudden the pace changed. Instead of being forced to stand still, Richard was ordered to start walking. 'Walk!' Richard tried to pull on his shoes but his feet were too swollen.

Twelve paces all round. Four steps for one wall, then two, four steps then two. Richard shuffled round in his socks. The guard would keep an eye on him through the spyhole. Occasionally orders would be shouted.

'Speed up.'

'Turn around.'

'Go in the other direction you idiot!'

'Faster!'

Richard stumbled, picking himself up while still moving. Four steps, then two. Four steps, then two. Moving, moving, moving, on, on, on, but never, ever, ever, getting anywhere. Hours went by. Richard desperately needed water, food, something to eat. Dehydration, caused by total absence of any fluid, along with a strong debilitating hunger followed Richard round the cell, four steps then two, four steps then two.

Richard spent days and nights moving round and round in an endless swirl of four by two, four by two. As he moved he prayed for the guards. The movements became more and more like a dance for Richard. Four steps, then two. Four steps, then two. As his mind revolved around the room everything else started to move as well. The whole cell seemed to join in with a never-ending dance of divine love. Walls merged with each other. Richard could not distinguish one end of the room from the other.

'What wall was that, that I just passed? I can't make out where the door is. It's all one. One long wall. It is just as divine love does not distinguish between good and evil men but can embrace everyone ... help me embrace everyone my Lord, my love. I will move with as much grace as if this were a dance for you, a dance of love for you.'

... and Richard danced, four by two, four by two.

Solitary Silence

Grey-faced, sagging skin, Richard Wurmbrand sat squatting in the corner of his cell. A month had passed and he had had no sleep. The most rest he got was what he was grabbing at that moment – a quick squat in the corner when no one was looking. When his mind was focused enough to realise that nobody was watching him the release of not being surveyed and scrutinised was immense. Every moment of every day was a continual peep-show, and Richard the curiosity.

'Animals at the zoo are treated better. I would love to be at the zoo right now,' Richard wished.

But just at the point when things can't get any worse the Communists would pull another perversion out of the hat. This was one of these moments.

Richard jumped to attention as a guard marched into the cell.

'ATTENTION! Stand up straight! QUICK, MARCH!'

The silence, the peace, that was so fragile was torn away. Richard was marched to another cell where a hood was pulled over his head. Richard was spread over a metal bar, tied up, and suspended from the ceiling. Hanging there over the metal bar, Richard felt like a trussed-up chicken. The whole experience was like a nightmare beginning to happen – then it did. A hand held Richard in a strangle hold round his neck while another took a leather whip and flogged the soles of his feet. That was only the start. Crack, the whip came down across his bare flesh, then on his spine, his shoulders, every place that was tender and sensitive. Richard fainted, but was quickly revived by drenchings of ice-cold water.

'Give us the names we want, who do you know, who were you working with? Just tell us and we will stop.'

That was all they wanted. But it was just what Richard would never give them. The torture didn't work but the torturers didn't give up. The more Richard fought, the more violent and perverse the torture. A knife was held to his throat, it pierced the skin. Richard fainted, waking up to find his chest covered in blood. Water was force-fed down his gullet until his belly was sore to the touch, then guards came in and stamped on him, hitting him full in the stomach.

In the end Richard agreed to sign whatever confessions they wanted about himself. He even said he was an adulterer and a homosexual, that he had sold the church bells and pocketed the money. But Richard's church had never even had a bell.

The torturers asked for more names. Names of Richard's friends, contacts, 'fellow revolutionaries'.

Richard handed over a long list of names.

Delighted, the authorities returned him to his cell. The pastor had cracked.

'They all do in the end. Couldn't stomach it. Just the right amount of pressure and you can squash them like soft grapes.' That was the considered opinion of the Secret Police.

However Richard's list was not so great once they took a second look at it.

'A. Valescu.'	'Dead.'
'D. Iova.'	'Exile.'
'F. Georgescu.'	'Prisoner of the State.'
'G. Patrascanu.'	'Dead.'
'T. Bajenaru.'	'Exile.'

... and so it went on. But the days that followed the big hoax gave Richard some much needed respite.

When the torture sessions started once more Richard had recovered a little, but then the pain started again.

Every torture session had a doctor present. When the prisoner fainted the doctor would come in, take his pulse and do all he could to revive the prisoner, so that the torture could begin again in earnest. No prisoner was allowed to escape into the next world when the Secret Police still had need of him. Richard felt that the whole procedure smarted of eternal punishment.

'It is like hell, where people are tormented and never allowed to die.'

In between torture sessions, Richard would try to remember Bible verses – just for a little bit of comfort or strength before the next round. However, this was getting more and more difficult.

'Um, ah, yes – Oh no, I used to know that verse, now how does it go?'

Richard's memory, his mind, the functions of the brain were being worn down by the endless torture.

'Why don't you just give in, tell us what we want to know? You are only flesh and blood after all and it won't be long until we break you completely!'

But Richard reminded himself that there was much more to it than that. 'If I was just flesh I could never have resisted this long, but my body is only a temporary residence for my soul. The Communists think man will do anything to avoid extinction, but I know different. Death is not the end of my life, only its fulfilment.'

* * *

Time marched on and the seasons changed. Richard sat shivering in the cold October breeze. It blew steadily through the window, chilling to the bone.

'I have spent a total of seven months surrounded by prison walls and winter is coming in fast.'

As he sat shivering he even looked forward to his plate of cold soup and hard bread, but he could hardly believe it when, instead, a beautiful plate of savoury goulash was placed in front of him.

Richard grabbed his fork and dived in. Not even one mouthful was chewed and swallowed when guards marched into the cell and handcuffed Richard. A gag was placed over his mouth and a blindfold over his eyes. He was being shifted again. All Richard could think of was his goulash.

'Couldn't I have a little bit more?'

But no, the beautiful food, the lovely savoury goulash had just been a cruel trick. It had never been meant for him, a prisoner.

Richard marched down the corridor, cold, confused and still hungry, the smell of savoury goulash haunting his nostrils.

A truck waited outside the prison walls and Richard joined a line-up of other prisoners all awaiting the same fate – the Ministry of the Interior. After a quick drive through the Bucharest streets Richard was off-loaded behind the walls of the magnificent Interior building and transported down below to the underground prison cells.

Richard remembered how tourists often admired the beautiful building from the outside.

'If they knew that it is built over an extensive prison with a labyrinth of corridors and hundreds of helpless inmates their reaction might be quite different!'

Another door slammed and Richard was in another cell, deep underground, bare and cold, with no window. Richard took one look around his cell – a lightbulb shone from the ceiling, bare walls reflected the gleam, an iron bedstead with three planks and a straw mattress sat in the corner of the room. A further look to the left showed Richard an iron pipe which looked as if it might have been an air-vent. Richard peered in all the other corners and under the bed just in case. With no place else to look Richard realised '... there is no bucket.'

'This is going to be awkward. They will stop at nothing, just to inflict a little bit more discomfort, embarrassment, indignity!'

Richard had been in prison long enough to realise that without a bucket he would have to rely on the guards to take him to the toilet to relieve himself. Richard had also been in prison long enough to realise that guards didn't always comply with a prisoner's requests. The guards would sometimes feel in the need of a bit of amusement and so would just sit and laugh at prisoners pleading pathetically to be taken to the toilet.

Over the following weeks Richard had to suffer this indignity.

'Please just let me go to the toilet. Five minutes that's all it will take.'

'Ha ha!' a guard would snigger. 'I think that one is going to burst at any moment, come and watch!'

On occasion Richard would have no choice but to use his own cell as a toilet. He would be so desperate that he would use his own eating bowl as a lavatory. To avoid the pain prisoners would even go without food and water.

Guards would poke fun at the poor prisoners who could just not hold on any longer. Soiled clothing, dirty skin, smelly cells. Lying around in their own urine and excrement – the prisoners felt inhuman, disgusting, worthless. The guards thought it was all an hilarious joke!

Richard felt he was shrinking inside. Everything was geared towards decreasing the prisoner, making him worthless in his own eyes, denying him any expression, any interest, any escape of any kind. All the doors were muffled so when they closed there was no sound. Complete, deliberate silence.

"There is no sound here, nothing, it's like death. Even the guards walk around in felt shoes. I feel like screaming out to give my ears something to listen to.'

Sitting, staring at the glaring lightbulb Richard tried to conjure up all the sounds he missed.

'I would love to hear the rain hitting against the stone pavement, the wind in the trees – how does it go? – swooosh, swooosh. The wind can be gentle, weaving in and out of the branches – then violent – crashing the waves against the seashore.

A fly buzzing in the corner of my cell – once an annoying sound. I would welcome it now.

My stomach used to rise up into my throat every time I heard steel boot-studs hitting against the corridor – 'Are they coming to get me this time?' I would ask. Even some boot-studs would break this deadening quiet.

But how I love hearing a human voice. Not the voices of these guards round here – they seem less than human sometimes. I long to hear the voice of a child laughing, just a quiet whisper from someone who cares, even a polite conversation about the weather, about how the wind is blowing outside and how the rain is falling on the mown grass. Yes, I miss the sounds of the wind, the rain ... what do they sound like again? Try and remember ... Oh! My heart is shrinking in this lifeless silence!'

Time passed. Two years in fact. Richard was kept in the cell for two years with no human contact, no fellow prisoners, no communication with anybody outside his four walls. Guards came and went silently as ever, more like shadows than people.

Richard fought a daily battle with tedium and silence. With nothing to read, no pens or paper to write with he had only his thoughts for company. Richard found this hard at first as he had never been one to dwell on things, to think or meditate or chew things over in his mind.

'I am not a meditative man,' Richard admitted to himself. 'In fact, I have to confess that my soul has rarely known quiet. No books, no writing, no sound. What have I got? I have God.'

Richard however had great doubts about this.

'How can I say I have God? Have I really lived to serve him, or is this "I have God" just words and nothing more?'

Pacing round his cell Richard battled with his doubts, fears, and self-criticism. He tried to get some meaning back into the silence.

'So often I have seen myself being raised up on to a

kind of pedestal. He's a pastor, he must be so wise, a man of God full of love, truth, purity. But I am also a man, not just a pastor. So many people expect so much so have I just given it to them? Is all my life just one big play act, a part in some make-believe scene – is any of the life I lived genuine? The question is do I believe in God?'

Mumbling to himself Richard let his thoughts wander round the question for a bit.

'Do I believe in God? I suppose being in this cell, with no friends, no family, no salary to earn, nobody else's opinions to consider is a test. God's test for me to put my stamp where it really matters. Do I believe in God when I have nothing else? God is offering me only suffering – do I still love him?'

The nights and days merged into a long line of time throughout which Richard lived to answer that question.

'God – Do I still love him?'

Richard slowly learned that the silence was a gift from God.

'The best preachers possessed an inner silence, like Jesus. When your mouth is open too much, even to speak good, the soul loses its fire just as a room loses its warmth through an open door.'

Breathing deeply Richard renewed his commitment to the Lord.

'I must make sure that I belong to him, that I belong to Christ.'

And as the nights and days merged into a long line of time, Richard passed that time in prayer and praise.

'This is not fiction, this is not a play-act. I believe that I believe!'

Even when there was nothing but prison, nothing but torture, Richard loved God because God loved Richard.

71

Dancing and leaping and praising God

'Aahh, no! no! Go away!'. Richard woke up from a fitful sleep. He had been tossing and turning on the straw mattress fighting off strange dreams of Brinzaru in his cavern of torture. Richard shook himself awake and he started to get ready for his programme.

Richard had not been in his new cell long when he realised that he required some sort of routine to keep his mind and body in working order. The key to Richard's programme was to stay awake all night. When the bell rang at 10 pm signalling time to sleep, Richard would get up and move about a bit working himself into the correct frame of mind. Sometimes Richard would be sad, sometimes cheerful but whatever mood he was in, the night never seemed long enough for everything Richard planned to do.

'There are just not enough hours in the night!'

Prayers of tears and thankfulness poured out from his soul. Richard often reminded himself, 'Prayers, like radio signals, are heard more clearly by night: it is then that great spiritual battles are fought.'

Richard knew that in the silence of the night God did not necessarily hear better but that Richard prayed better. With most of the guards and prisoners asleep he was alone to enjoy uninterrupted communication with his Creator.

After prayer Richard preached. Standing up, he would imagine himself in front of a congregation and start as usual with: '*Beloved Brethren....*'

Only in prison Richard whispered his sermon – even at night Richard could not risk alerting one of the guards.

Richard would then proceed with his thoughts for the evening. Never before had he felt such freedom in preaching. He no longer had to think about what *people* thought. Richard preached to his heart's content. It was wonderful.

But he wasn't preaching to thin air. Conscious that his Lord and Saviour was with him at all times Richard realised that every sermon was heard by him. As he preached Richard felt the presence of others as well – angels, saints dead and alive, friends and family. They were all there.

'I feel so many listeners present in this room. We will all worship God together in the beauty of holiness.'

It was amazing. Richard felt surrounded by people, all listening to his sermons, though he couldn't see anybody.

Years later Richard found out about other listeners – a young criminal in solitary confinement in a Canadian jail repented and believed the gospel because he heard and saw Richard Wurmbrand preaching from his prison cell in Romania. A woman in England experienced the same situation and a young man in France came to know the Lord as a result of the same sermons. None of them were in the cell, none of them were in the same country, all heard the same sermons and believed.

As part of the nightly routine Richard kept up contact with his family. Every night there was a family time for Richard, Sabina, and little Mihai. It didn't feel strange, just natural and right.

'Ah Sabina, how are you tonight? I love you darling, you are all I could have ever wished for in a wife. Little Mihai, such a clever little boy you are, you will have grown so much since I last saw you. I don't think I would know you if I saw you. I will see you one day – soon I hope. Maybe you don't like being called a little boy, now that you are growing up?'

Richard would reminisce with his family about happier times.

'There was that time when Mihai was out playing in the park. Sabina, remember, we were walking just a little bit behind him. Well, I couldn't believe it when he walked straight up to that stranger sitting on the bench and asked him, 'What are you reading sir?'

'A novel,' he said. I think he was a little bit surprised.

'You had better read the Bible,' Mihai replied. 'Go and speak to my mum and dad, that's them over there.'

The man was so struck by Mihai's little speech that he came up to us and started asking us questions. It's amazing to think of him now, one of God's children. Mihai, you were a good little evangelist even back then!'

One evening as Richard was thinking of Sabina he had quite a surprising thought.

'Perhaps I can speak to Sabina, really speak to her, even from behind these prison walls?'

Richard believed that if he felt it passionately enough, if his mind tried hard enough, with God's help he could reach Sabina. Suddenly it was as if the prison walls fell away and Richard was standing over Sabina in her room. She opened her eyes and looked straight into his face. They had made it – just for a few seconds they were together in mind and spirit.

74

'I love you.'
'I love you.'
That was all.
It was all they needed.

* * *

During the day-time Richard would sleep a little if allowed and spend the rest of the time trying to keep his mind occupied in any way he could. Lying back he would allow his mind to wander to places far and wide.

'I wonder what it would be like to be a grand emperor in China? I would sit on a big throne with thousands of servants to do my bidding. I would not be spoken to without great respect and honour. Even princes and kings from far away lands would come and admire my palaces, and lands. Yes I can see myself sitting on my throne right now, dressed in silks and a huge turban. I wonder if I would look a bit silly? No, emperors do not look silly, they are grand and regal.'

'Now, if I could fly where would I go? Out of here for a start, straight home to Sabina. If I were to sprout wings here and now I would fly up through the ceiling – a bit difficult? Well, if I was outside I would sprout wings, and shoot off up over the prison walls into the wide blue yonder. I wonder what it is like flying through a cloud? With my wings I could sit on top of one and look down below – no body could touch me up there – just me and the birds.'

On a more serious note Richard would save pieces of bread and make up a chess board. Only he had no one to play against so he played both the black and white pieces. Except the pieces were made up from black and less black bread. One good thing about playing against yourself at chess is that you always win every game. Richard smiled at the thought of not losing a game in two years.

* * *

The door quickly opened, and a silent guard placed another dish of dry bread down on the floor.

Richard woke up after a few minutes sleep to another prison breakfast which enabled him to work out that it was indeed another day.

Sighing, he reminded himself to rejoice and be glad and then he remembered a verse, 'Oh – yes, there's that verse in Matthew – "Rejoice in that day and leap for joy". I should be leaping for joy. I have only been obeying half of this command. I must leap, I must!'

Richard started to leap, and prance, and jump all around his cell. From one foot to the other he leapt and bounded about. The prison cell took on new life as Richard praised the Lord in a flurry of movement.

Hearing the commotion a guard peeked through the spyhole.

'What on earth? Help! He is going mad! I'd better do something.'

The guard rushed off in a flurry of movement himself and shot back with some extra rations of food – more food and better food than Richard had seen in a long time.

Fresh bread, cheese and sugar.

Richard tucked in, remembering the rest of that verse, 'Rejoice in that day and leap for joy – for behold your reward is great.' Richard noted that it was indeed a very large piece of bread, more than a week's ration!

Every night was spent dancing from then on but Richard was never paid for it again. The guards just got used to the strange goings on and ignored him. But Richard continued to dance in thankfulness and praise to God.

* * *

'Tap tap tap.'

Richard jumped up again for the third time that evening.

'Where is that sound coming from?'

Shuffling over to the wall again, he listened hard.

'Tap tap tap.'

'There it is again, and I think its coming from through the wall.'

Richard raised his hand and tapped back.

'Tap tap tap.'

He waited and sure enough, 'Tap tap tap tap.'

Richard replied, 'Tap tap tap tap.'

'A new prisoner must have arrived next door and he is trying to signal to me.'

Richard's reply provoked a flurry of fresh taps. It didn't take long for Richard to realise that the new prisoner was trying to convey a code to him.

A= 1 tap, B = 2 taps, C = 3 taps, and so on.

'Who are you?' was the stranger's first message.

Slowly but surely Richard tapped out his reply.

'A pastor.'

The communication system worked fine but soon Richard and his friend were trying new systems to improve on the old one till eventually Richard's friend taught him Morse code.

One night Richard asked his friend, 'Are you a Christian?'

After a long pause a reply came through.

'I cannot claim that.'

Throughout the night the man shared his story.

'I was a radio engineer before I was imprisoned here. I married someone who did not believe in Jesus. That was what made me fall away. I used to believe years ago.'

Night after night they talked through the wall. Richard realised that the man was very depressed and burdened. One night Richard heard the tapping again.

'Please, I should like to confess my sins.'

The radio engineer unburdened his sins and troubles. When he was a young boy he had hit a school friend, the school friend had turned to him and said – 'Your mother will die alone!' – an unusual thing to say but while he was in prison his mother had died and he hadn't been there to help her.

Richard taught him Bible verses and stories, encouraging him and strengthening him. The two became not pen-friends but Morse-friends. They even played chess games through the wall. Most importantly Richard passed on messages about Christ.

'He loves you, you know. He died for you and took the punishment for your sins. All you have to do is turn to him, ask him to help you. There is nothing more – he is everything you need. He can help you to banish sin from your life. You can return to a life that honours God. A clean, fresh start!'

However, one night Richard was tapping away and

the silent felt shoes of a guard crept up on him.

'Ah ha! What is this we have here! Communicating with other prisoners is forbidden.'

Richard was immediately transferred to another prison cell.

In the new prison cell, Richard went over to the wall.

'Tap tap tap,' he rapped his knuckles on the cement wall and started again with the next prisoner.

***

Richard yawned. It was morning again and he had just spent another night in prayer and praise. Exhausted he was just about to finish a bit of dried bread and try and sleep for a few minutes.

'Tap tap tap.'

Richard woke up, and dashed over to the wall.

'Tap tap tap.'

Messages flew back and forward and Richard learned that today was Good Friday. Easter was here. Happy and thankful Richard praised the Lord and tried to think of a way in which he could spread this joy to other prisoners. On a visit to the lavatory, Richard caught a glimpse of a nail just hidden in a corner in a pile of dust. When the guard wasn't looking he hid it under his sleeve and then he was taken back to the cell.

'How can I use this little nail to spread God's love and joy at Easter?' Pausing for a minute Richard scratched his head in concentration. Then it struck him.

'I will write Jesus' name on my cell wall. That means whoever comes here after me will find a little bit of joy and encouragement here.'

Taking the nail he slowly scratched 'JESUS' on his

cell wall, then stood back to admire it. The scratching on the wall must have attracted the attention of one of the guards as someone soon came along to investigate.

Seeing the name of Jesus the guard was infuriated.

'You're for the Carcer!'

Richard knew only too well what this meant. The Carcer was a tall thin box where people were locked up as a form of prison punishment. Richard was thrust in and the door was locked. Sharp nails dug into his back. Richard leaned forward to get his back away from the spikes only to lean against nails that stuck into his front. Richard began to panic.

'Maybe I can move to the side?' Feeling his hands gently up the sides of the Carcer, Richard felt even more needles and spikes sticking out, piercing, cutting.

'If I faint, or fall into these spikes they'll go right through me.'

Pitch dark, totally alone, not able to move and pain on every side, there was nothing to be done but force yourself to stand still.

'My legs, oh, my legs. It's so sore.' Richard groaned as stabs of pain shot up his thigh. An hour had passed and every muscle began to hurt. Richard's feet had never quite recovered from the previous torture and his ankles slowly began to swell up.

Not long afterwards Richard collapsed against the nails. His skin was lacerated and bleeding, the nails dug into his flesh cutting deeper and deeper. The guards quickly dragged him out of the Carcer and left him on the floor to recuperate. Opening his eyes Richard slowly came back to the land of the living and realised he was out of the Carcer at last.

'Look, he's awake.' A guard pointed at the prostrate figure of Richard lying on the cold slabs.

'Put him back in then,' replied the other.

Heaving his broken and bleeding body up off the cold stone floor the guards flung Richard back inside the torture box.

The torture disturbed Richard so deeply he found that even his mind shut itself off. Richard tried to keep his mind on Christ's sufferings but his own sufferings kept getting stronger and stronger so that even this source of encouragement seemed to dry up.

'Heavenly Father what can I do? I can't keep it up, I'm giving up Lord, I can't keep going.'

Richard's mind wandered, dreams came and went – reality merged with fiction as Richard fought hard to keep conscious. Thinking about Mihai, Richard remembered one early spring morning how he had been sitting in his study and had heard a quiet little knock on the door.

'Daddy.' Mihai bounced in. 'I'm bored. What shall I do Daddy?'

'Think about God, Mihai.'

Mihai replied, 'Why? I have only a small head. God has a great big head. He should think about me instead.'

Richard smiled at the child's wisdom and consoled himself with its truth.

'Don't try to think about God. Don't think at all. Jesus is thinking of me, he will surround me and protect me. Lord Jesus have mercy upon me, Lord Jesus have mercy upon me. Jesus, dear bridegroom of my soul, I love you. Jesus, dear bridegroom of my soul, I love you. Lord Jesus have mercy upon me, Lord Jesus have mercy upon me.'

Soon the calm nature of the words, the soothing peace of his prayer numbed his thoughts giving him relief. Richard ceased to think.

Richard retreated his mind far away from everything – cutting himself off completely for two whole days.

* * *

The doctor came and gave Richard a quick examination.

'You had better get that prisoner out of the Carcer, or you are going to lose him. His condition has become dangerous – I recommend immediate withdrawal.'

After two days Richard was released. This in itself was a miracle as many prisoners had to endure this form of torture for a week or more. But Richard was in a no-man's-land between the living and the dead. The authorities still believed they had much to gain from keeping this pastor alive. For their own sakes and not for Richard's comfort they withdrew him back to his cell.

* * *

Richard came to as he was flung onto the straw mattress. His eyes flickered as he came to in his old cell. Confused, he muttered something to himself but soon collapsed again into a frantic world of dreams and fantasies.

Sweating profusely and in a fit of coughing Richard would wake up from these nightmares and force himself to stay awake.

'If I stare long enough at my cup of water I will convince myself that I am not in Hell. There is not even a drop of water in Hell.'

But as he stared at his cup of water it changed into strange and peculiar things. Richard lived in a mad world where nothing was what it seemed and where there was no reality. Delicious dishes were laid out before him on a massive banqueting table that stretched way off into the distance far beyond his little cell. Sabina appeared from nowhere with a plate of sausages and uncharacteristically Richard snarled at her. 'What? Is that all? How small and puny these sausages are!'

Suddenly the banqueting table disappeared, Sabina sped off in the other direction with the sausages and Richard was back in his cell, alone and shivering, just waiting for the next hallucination.

It wasn't long in coming. Richard closed his eyes and then opened them.

'What? Where did all these books come from?'

Rows and rows of books had taken the place of the banqueting table. They stretched as far as his eye could see and climbed high up the wall, through the ceiling and possibly even to the sky. Books were everywhere. Famous novels, poetry, biographies, religious and scientific works, towered above him. Richard strained his neck to look at row upon row of all of his old favourites. Richard blinked and all the books changed into thousands of faces staring expectantly at him as if waiting for him to say something earth-shattering, important, vital! All the faces shouted questions at each other and other faces answered back. A mass of voices and faces shouting and cheering, stretching out and out into infinity.

As quickly as the faces came the faces went and Richard lay back exhausted. Sleep came eventually but it was troubled. Richard dreamt of violence and revenge. In his dream a guard came into the cell and Richard pounced on him pummelling him into the hard concrete floor until he was no more. A long grey corridor shot out through the wall of his cell and, running, he followed it wherever it turned shoving guards and interrogators out of the way – throwing them down stairs, kicking them, lashing out for every time they had lashed out at him.

Richard fought hard to resist the hallucinations, the thirst for violence. The only way he could win this particular battle was to imagine it as just that – a battle.

'This thirst for violence is an enemy, I must fight it. The hallucinations creep up on me, camouflaged, ready to strike. I must be smart, cunning, and work out a way to send them packing.'

Richard sat and thought a little, not fighting off the dreams and nightmares but letting them stay a bit while he pondered what to do about them.

'These dreams and evil thoughts will ultimately bring my ruin. If I give into these temptations they will destroy my life and the life of my family. If I let these evil lustful thoughts run riot in my life I will have to divorce my wife, my son will disown me and all my parishioners will be ashamed of me.' This fear of disgrace and failure helped Richard fight the evil that threatened to ruin him.

* * *

A guard marched Richard along the corridor to the prisoner's lavatory. The stink that wafted out from behind the door hinted at only one thing.

'The lavatory is blocked.' The guard cursed. 'I'm not going in there. I'll have to take you to the guard's lavatory.'

Shuffling along the corridor to the other lavatory,

Richard was relieved the guard hadn't just shoved him back in his cell to wet himself.

Richard, curious at what he might find, took a quick look around him. A washbasin, clean and sparkling and toilets that didn't smell. Richard turned quickly as something clean and shiny caught the corner of his eye.

'Its a mirror,' he said, whispering. The guard, busy for a minute, polished a bit of dust from off his shoe. Richard stood for a second in front of the mirror. It had been years since he had seen himself in a looking-glass. Dazed and rather surprised he gasped at the man he saw.

'Who is that? Is it me? I used to be young. I used to look strong and healthy. Why, I believe people used to call me handsome? That old wrinkled man is me. Grey-faced, tired, no hair. Where has all my colour gone? I look like pale porridge. So old, just so old...' Richard laughed, silently to himself. Though what there was to laugh about he didn't know.

'It's sad really. Pathetic. Look at me. People used to admire me and look up to me. What would they think now if they saw this tired, frightened old man? This has taught me a lesson. I look far too much on what the eye sees. I must learn that what makes a person really beautiful is invisible to the eye. It is loving God and loving others that makes you beautiful.'

Sitting down on the toilet Richard picked up a torn piece of newspaper from off the ground.

'It's been so long since I read a newspaper.' Richard sat back for a few seconds to lap up this little bit of luxury.

The main title read: '*President Groza has firmly decided to wipe out the rich.*'

Chuckling to himself Richard saw the ridiculousness

of the idea.

'Groza, the Romanian President, is trying to wipe out the rich when the rest of the world fights poverty!'

Richard jumped as the guards voice boomed outside in the corridor.

'Hey you! Have you finished in there – you're taking too long, get a move on.'

Richard pulled up his baggy old pants and shot out of the toilet. It was best not to be caught reading a newspaper. Who knows? It might have earned him another trip to the Carcer.

Smiling to himself as he sat down on his mattress Richard was relieved that he had finally got to read something, and it wasn't an hallucination.

'It just feels so good. Reading, a simple pleasure. Such a great privilege. Thank you, God!'

* * *

Things had been quieter than usual for a few days now and Richard began to wonder if something was up.

'Maybe they have forgotten about me.'

There had been no interrogations for quite a while, no questions asked, no trips blindfolded down long corridors. What was going on?

The spyhole clanked, and the door creaked on its hinges as it swung open.

'Prisoner, stand to attention! Lieutenant Grecu has requested your presence at the interrogation room. Quick march!'

'Thought it was too good to be true,' Richard muttered as he started off again down another long corridor.

Unmasked and sitting poker-straight on a tall stool,

Richard looked Lt. Grecu in the eye. A tough young man, confident and self-assured he stood returning Richard's stare eyeball to eyeball. He sincerely believed he was building a better world and that Richard was the enemy.

He fired questions about Richard's charity work and famine relief.

'Admit it. You used the money for spying and espionage! It wasn't for famine relief at all, you trickster!'

At the next meeting Richard was questioned about Russian gospels and mission work. Not wishing to name anyone Richard passed on a name of a Russian pastor who had died three years ago. At the next meeting Richard was shouted at for trying to fool his interrogator.

'Your story was lies! Lies!! Enough, you will write everything on this paper. Who you are secretly communicating with in jail? What they are saying to you? All the prison rules you are breaking – tell us everything.'

The truncheon came down, whack, on the table.

'If you don't...' Lt. Grecu stroked the truncheon. It lay in his hands, polished, gleaming, and poised to strike. Glaring at Richard, Grecu left the room and with an, 'I'll be back,' he slammed the door.

Richard picked up the pen and gingerly started moving it across the paper.

'It must have been over two years now since I held a pen. I can't have forgotten how to use it?'

But after a troubled start Richard eventually managed to scrawl some sort of confession.

I have tapped out the gospel message through the prison walls.
I have hoarded sleeping-pills in order to kill myself.

I made a knife out of a piece of tin.
I play chess with pieces of bread.
I have never spoken against the Communists. I am a
Christian, a disciple of Christ and he has given me
love for my enemies. I understand Communists and
pray for their conversion; so that they will become
my brothers in the Faith.'

Grecu marched back into the room, confidently swinging his truncheon. Reaching down he picked up the confession and began to read. After a while he looked across at Richard.

'He looks troubled?' Richard thought.

Grecu coughed, clearing his throat and addressing Richard he asked, 'Why do you say that you love me? This is just one of those Christian commandments that it is impossible to keep. I couldn't love someone who shut me up for years, alone, starved and beaten.'

'It's not a matter of keeping a commandment. When I became a Christian it was as if I had been reborn, with a new character which was full of love. Just as only water can flow from a spring, so only love can come from a loving heart.'

Two hours passed where the only topic of conversation was Christianity.

'Karl Marx said that Christianity – is "the ideal religion for the remaking of a life destroyed by sin". My life was destroyed by sin. When I follow Jesus I am just following Karl Marx's advice. In fact, Karl Marx's first book was on St. John's gospel. Interesting isn't it?' Richard Wurmbrand had found a surprising listener to the good news of the gospel. Day after day Richard was requested to attend Lt. Grecu's interrogations. Day after day Richard and the Lieutenant discussed Christianity.

Weeks went by with Richard discussing and debating and Lt. Grecu questioning and listening. Richard prayed for wisdom and was given it. He didn't lash out at the Communists but pointed out their good points. Richard showed how Lt. Grecu wasn't so far away from following Jesus himself. Lt. Grecu listened intently. Gradually the words went into his heart.

'I want to confess my sins. I love Jesus. Will you pray with me?'

Kneeling down on the floor, one in a suit, the other in prison rags, Grecu and Wurmbrand became brothers in Christ.

* * *

From that point on Lt. Grecu bravely helped the prisoners wherever he could. But one day something happened that changed all that.

Tap tap tap. A Morse code message came through Richard's wall.

'What is it?' he tapped back.

'Grecu. Disappeared, presumed arrested.'

Richard sighed. 'If you really love Jesus you just can't hide it!'

Dear Jesus

Richard sat, ashen-faced in the corner of the cell, coughing up blood.

'Its been nearly three years now. Three years alone – but alone with you Jesus.'

Coughing set in again, blood seeped out from between his fingers. His hands trembled, as they moved across an imaginary sheet of paper. His fingers clasped around a pen that only he could see. His mind composed letters, long and probing letters, soft and worshipful ones, powerful prose and quiet poetry.

'Dear Jesus,

The first thing I want to tell you is the simple truth, I love you. I love pudding, I love a dog, I love people, I love you. I have to use the same word because of the poverty of language. There is simply no adequate expression for the sentiment I have for you. So let me conclude with this: you are my love. ... The fact is, I was once a crucifier, till an encounter with your all-forgiving love changed me. If I could be transformed, others can too. I will dedicate my life to this.'

Other letters cried out in anguish:

'Father! The Communists suffer too. A Communist officer was in the basement of the Secret Police headquarters with a mass of corpses, the men he had just shot. He began to cry aloud, as he went from corpse to corpse: "Please say something! Move! I did not mean to do you ill. I did not even know you. I shot you, but did

not desire that you be so completely dead for ever. Please speak! Please move!" His comrades first put him in an asylum, then, to silence their own conscience, finished him off.

The pain of this criminal is also mine. To be very honest with you, I must say there is in me a voice that says "I hate God" because of this tragedy. I do not silence this voice, fearing that if it is repressed it will become louder.

... Millions are without a crust of bread. ... We meet temptations every day, and we are not delivered from evil. Why? What is wrong? It is hard for me to continue this letter today. Farewell till another time.'

The anguished cry would then be followed by a beautiful apology:

'Dear Jesus,

I broke off my last letter on a very sore point. I had even gone so far as to say, "I hate God".

We have a good God and a bad world... We are the ones that fail you God. We don't obey you. Now you, Jesus, continue with your work of peace making, though much of your loving energy has been squandered, but you are love and love continues to strive. Love doesn't give up.'

Richard's letter-writing was just another way to speak with Jesus. Richard received answers to his prayers which he treated like letters of reply. Each one he treasured like a jewel and painstakingly saved in his memory.

'Maybe one day I will write all these letters down in a book, all the questions, the anger, the frustration, the love, the tears and the answers. It has been the only thing that has kept me sane! I shouldn't wonder that talking

with you Lord has kept me sane – it's no surprise!'
Richard smiled as he withdrew into his mind and soul
retrieving past promises, reliving past blessings, and
looking forward to a future of eternal love.

Another fit of coughing brought him back to the
present reality of time and torture.

'I remember the prison officer yesterday sneering at
me, "We are not murderers like the Nazis. We want you
to live ... and suffer!" Lord how I am suffering now.
This cough is killing me.'

And it was, Richard's health was deteriorating rapidly.
To the Communists he was still valuable and a specialist
was called.

The specialist came up to the spyhole and peered in.
Covering his mouth with a handkerchief he made it
abundantly clear he was not about to catch whatever it
was that Richard had.

Without even coming through the door the specialist
signed a form, closed the spyhole and ordered that
Richard be taken to the prison hospital.

'Immediately.'

Rushing off down the corridor the doctor disappeared
as if a whole army of germs were hot on his heels.

Richard lay doubled over on the floor. Another
coughing fit had started. Simple scripture texts that had
not quite faded from his memory swam around in the
confusion of his mind.

'Our Father, that art in heaven, hallowed be thy name.
Thy kingdom come ... *when is your kingdom coming
Lord? When?* Thy will be done ... *here? Your will being
done here?* In earth as it is in heaven.... *Oh to be in heaven
with you Lord Jesus, to be home.*'

'Give us this day our daily bread.'

The guards come in. One takes hold of an arm, another takes hold of his legs. Richard is swung on to a stretcher.

'... and forgive us our debts, as we forgive our debtors ... *Lord, help me to forgive them. Help me to love the sinner but hate the sin ...*'

Richard's stretcher is carted out of the cell and down the corridor.

'And lead us not into temptation, but deliver us from evil ... *deliver me oh Lord from this evil present all around me* ... For thine is the Kingdom, the power and the glory for ever and ever, Amen.'

With that Richard was taken from the prison and into a large, outdoor courtyard.

Looking up, he gasped, 'Beautiful, so beautiful.'

Millions upon millions of stars, shone, clean and pure. The sky was pitch-dark all around except for the pin-pricks of piercing light.

'Lord, thank you for the stars, I haven't seen them in over three years!'

The sky vanished from sight as Richard's stretcher was pushed into the back of a van. Lying back coughing in the stretcher Richard stared out of the side-window at streets, shops, schools and restaurants. People made their way home from a night at the movies. Lovers walked hand in hand. Lights went out in homes all over Bucharest. Richard Wurmbrand lay cold and shivering, coughing up blood, and just longing to go home.

'Wait,' Richard took a quick look at his surroundings. 'That's the butchers shop a few streets from home. Why, we're turning up that road that has the grocers on it. There's Jacob's house and the school. If we carry on and turn right, I will be home! Are they taking me home? Home to die?'

Richard's eyes brightened in anticipation. The longing for home, the ache to hold Sabina and Mihai, the pain of being alone for so very, very long. It was all too much for him. Tears pricked his eyes, seeping down the wrinkles of his face.

'Please, let me go home.' The hoarse whisper of a tired man was not heard by any of the guards. If they had heard it they would have enjoyed a good joke. But as it was the van drove on, and on. No right turns, no welcome home. No reunions, no loving arms. Richard lay back on his stretcher and let the tears fall on.

'Why did I let myself think I was going home? Going home? I'll never go home ... they'll never let me out ... never.'

The van shuddered as it turned the corner. Cobble-stones underneath the wheels drummed out a thundering roll. Each shake went straight through Richard, jarring every bone in his body. Turning up a hill Richard finally realised where it was they were taking him.

'Yes, this is Vacaresti, the prison hospital. I thought as much.'

The van stopped inside a courtyard and a sheet was quickly bound round his face. Gripped under the arms Richard half-walked and was half-carried across the courtyard, up some stairs and along a balcony.

The sheet was removed and Richard found himself, alone again. Alone again in a narrow, bare cell.

Outside the door, an order was given to a grey-suited guard.

'No one is allowed to see this man except the doctor,

and then you must be there as a witness.'

The guard stood to attention and saluted. A pair of boots was heard walking away and then the door of Richard's cell slowly opened. A puzzled pair of eyes studied Richard closely.

'What on earth have you done?' The puzzled pair of eyes stared even closer. Was this man a murderer, had he robbed the State Bank, perhaps he had grossly insulted the President? Whatever it was it was serious.

'I am a pastor and a child of God,' was Richard's reply.

The puzzled pair of eyes almost popped out of their sockets. That was different.

'Praise the Lord, I too am one of Christ's soldiers!'

Shaking Richard's wrinkled hand, he introduced himself.

'By the way, my name is Tachici.'

'Mine is Richard.'

Lying back on the bench, Richard closed his eyes to catch a few minutes sleep.

'What a joy to find a disciple amongst the guards! What a surprise!'

* * *

Week followed week and Richard coughed and coughed. Each cough seemed to sap out every last ounce of energy he had. Too weak to leave his bed Richard often lay there in his own mess until someone could bother to come and clean him up. Often nobody could be bothered to do anything about him. However, if Tachici was around he would come and help him clean up. On those occasions they would exchange Bible verses and short prayer times.

'Such a special delight are these times with you my friend.' Richard would grasp the guards strong hand in his weak frail one. Christian fellowship in a stronghold of Communism – definitely a blessing to be counted.

One thing that delighted Richard was the window.

'Its so good to have a window again. Real sunlight, real sounds. Oh, just listen to that bluetit singing its heart out. Wonderful!'

Sometimes the sound irritated him. This was difficult to understand.

'For so long I ached after the sound of a human voice. I longed to hear a whisper, a shout, just a voice. Now I hear the voices down in the courtyard – they talk about this and that, bits and pieces of nothing – and I get so irritated. I just want to shut them out!'

Finally Richard woke up one morning to a prison guard shaking him on the shoulder.

'You are to be tried in the state court today. So get up and get a move on.'

Richard was finally going to be tried. He was finally going to see some Romanian Justice. As he thought about this 'Romanian Justice' Richard had some serious doubts.

Later on that day he was marched in front of a panel of judges.

The charges were read, the cases made. Richard was forbidden any witnesses so his case didn't take long.

'Do you have anything to say?'

Richard paused. Then coughing he replied, 'I love God.'

'Twenty years hard labour. Case closed.'

* * *

Coughing racked his body. It never went away. For two days Richard lay down on the bench coughing continuously. Pondering the outcome of the case he wondered what would happen in twenty years.

"Mihai will be a grown man by then – maybe with children of his own. What will I be then – an old, tired man, certainly not the father he once knew. Of course, I may be dead by then, who knows? You know God, you know where I will be. I'll let you worry about it and I'll just concentrate on you.'

Tachici quickly entered Richard's cell and whispered anxiously in his ear.

'You're leaving, God be with you.' Richard was marched out yet again into the courtyard, on his way to yet another prison.

* * *

Maria Pappov stood silently in the long queue of prisoners. Her long brown hair had been cut short into a bob but she still reached up to her shoulder to fiddle with her hair – only to remember that it was no longer there.

'I'm so lonely, there is no one here who cares whether I live or die. I want to die. I'm so ashamed.' The last sentence she had muttered out loud. Realising her indiscretion Maria turned to see if anyone had heard, but no one was listening. Everyone else was absorbed in their own problems.

'Why did I do it? I'm disgraced.' Moist tears shone out from behind her light-brown eyes. Every day she seemed to relive the circumstances that had brought her to this place and every day she finished with the question

'Why did I do it? Why?'

The morning had been like many other mornings. She had walked through the market on her way to work – had it only been three weeks ago? Three weeks ago she had looked at all the things that she could not afford. Maria dreamt of a day when she and her parents could live and eat well, with no worries, no scrimping. 'I remember looking at the side of beef, the leather shoes, then seeing a warm winter coat. It was then ... that's when the thought came.' Maria had walked on, a little worm of a thought chewing away inside. She arrived at work ten minutes early, as usual. Her first job was checking the till at the department store that she worked in. Rich Communist's wives shopped for luxuries and perfumes, necessities such as food and clothing were bought without a second thought. After she came back from her break she looked at the cash sitting in the register and took a long, deep breath. 'Nobody will notice the money is missing. I'll say it was a mistake if they notice it. I gave someone the wrong change or something.' However, sharp eyes and a quick check of the till accounts made sure that she did not get away with it. A handful of notes and change and Maria was sentenced to several years hard labour. Her parents couldn't understand, her friends at church felt that there must have been some mistake. Maria stood moving down the prison queue and wished that the whole thing was a mistake – but it wasn't.

'Prison looks bad from here, but what will I do when I'm released? None of my friends will ever trust me. I'm a thief!'

Maria moved slowly down the line. 'So many have

been imprisoned for no reason. The pastor was imprisoned for his faith. If I had a faith like his would it make a difference? ... but I am just a common thief. My life's a mess. I am just a disgusting mess. God wouldn't look twice at me.'

A truck stood where the queue of prisoners was waiting to be processed and checked and marked off and marched in. Richard scrambled into the van just immediately after Maria. He was exhausted and barely managed to stay on his feet. He coughed and caught a glimpse of sympathy from the young woman in front of him, and then something struck him.

'What is it about that girl – she looks familiar – where would I have seen her before?'

Suddenly she turned away to look in the other direction. Her complexion paled, she looked horrified.

Maria's heart jumped into her throat the minute she saw Richard smiling at her from across the van. 'Oh no, it can't be, oh no. Please God, not this, not him. I've been humiliated enough, you know I won't do it again. Quick Maria hide! Where can I hide? Help! I can't speak to the pastor. He mustn't find out.'

As the van pulled out of the prison yard Maria's stomach tightened into a knot. There was no place to hide, no way out. Fervently she prayed that the pastor would not recognise her. But Richard had. Coughing slightly Richard tried to crack a joke, 'Another day another prison.' It didn't go down too well with the rest of the crew but, undeterred, Richard smiled and moved over to sit beside Maria.

'Good day child. I used to know you didn't I?'

Maria stared into the beautiful deep blue eyes. Hiding

99

the truth was impossible. It would be a relief to finally let it go – she had carried about this burden of guilt for far too long.

'Yes, Pastor Wurmbrand, I used to be in your church. My name is Maria, daughter of Mr. and Mrs. Pappov.'

Embarrassed she turned away. How was she going to tell this lovely old man. He would be so annoyed with her – she had sinned dreadfully. 'I remember he preached against Sin.' Her gaze remained buried in the sandy floor of the van. Richard was puzzled at her response.

'Why is she behaving in this way? I don't understand.'

Turning to her again, Richard coughed politely.

'If there is anyway I can help you please ask. There is something troubling you, what is it?'

Maria let it all rush out. All the pain, the shame, the disgrace that had rotted inside her for so long. 'You are here because of your faith. I am here because I am a thief. Pastor Wurmbrand, I am so ashamed. I wish I hadn't done it. I feel so ashamed. I'm a thief!' Tears flooded her face. It was so good to let go.

Richard held her hand. He smiled gently. What he said next was nothing short of surprising. Maria was struck dumb.

'I too am a sinner, saved by the grace of God. Believe in Christ and your sins will be forgiven.'

That was it. The van jerked to a stop – they had only travelled a few miles – but Maria had to get out along with the other women. She smiled, for the first time in months and stepped down onto the concrete road leading up to the women's labour camp.

'When I am released I will tell your family that I saw you.'

Maria turned and waved as the doors closed and Richard was driven off.

'I am glad I met her, Lord. I hope she meets you soon. Be with her. Strengthen her. Help her to bring news of me to Sabina.'

Maria walked on up the hill, her heart felt different, her mind felt different, her eyes felt different. She was different. 'I had forgotten about the forgiveness of sins, he preached about that too. What a relief. In a couple of years I will be out of here. It's so good to start from scratch. It is so good to be alive!'

* * *

The van slowed to a halt not too long after Richard had said goodbye to the young girl. A special wagon sat waiting at a railway siding ready to transport the prisoners to a special TB Prison. Conversation amongst the inmates had revealed that the one thing they had in common was the infectious TB virus. This virus was highly infectious and destroyed the lungs. That was why Richard was coughing so much.

Two hundred miles passed under the rattling rhythm of the old engine. One day and one night later they arrived at another station. The town of Tirgul Ocna, had 30,000 people, a railway station and a Communist jail. Richard lay on a hard stretcher as guards and officials busied about the wagons shoving the prisoners out of the train like cattle. Richard was among the ones that couldn't walk and had to wait until he could be carried off. Eventually they were thrown into the back of a cart and pulled up a hill by the other prisoners to the Tirgul Ocna jail.

The gates opened and the new stock shuffled in. Richard stared at the crowd of faces there waiting for them. Other inmates, guards, prison officers stared at the dishevelled crew. Amongst the sea of faces Richard spotted a familiar one.

'Dr. Aldea. Dr. Aldea. It's me, Richard Wurmbrand. How are you?'

The Doctor turned and smiled, recognising Richard even after all this time.

'Richard, how good it is to see you. I am well,' he caught his breath as he recognised the gravity of Richard's symptoms. 'But you, my friend, are not. I am sorry to say this but your health looks bad.' Dr. Aldea took Richard's pulse, and did a very thorough check-over.

'I am concerned about you Richard – for now you will be allotted a room in the quarantine area until it's decided what should be done about you. I'm a prisoner myself here but they let me work as a doctor. No nurses to speak of, and only one other physician. So the prisoners look after one another as best they can. Right ... Let me take a look at that." Holding a thermometer up Aldea took a quick glance and then muttered something. The temperature was high, dangerously high.

'Richard, I'm not going to deceive you. There's nothing we can do. All I can say is that you may have only two weeks to live. Try and eat what you can – the food you get here is not good but it's all you get. If you don't ... well...'

Aldea placed his hand on Richard's shoulder. There was a lump in his throat. Quickly he moved on to the next prisoner.

Richard lay back and tried not to dwell too much on what had been said, after all there was nothing that could be done.

'There is no use tying myself in knots over this. I'll just lie quiet for now.'

But lying quiet was virtually impossible when every moment of every day was spent coughing up blood.

New days passed and most of the other men that had been with Richard in the cart were dropping like flies. The majority of them were no longer in the quarantine room but placed in a room on their own. This room was called Room 4. If you had to talk about Room 4 you did so in hushed tones.

'He has been shifted to Room 4.'

'Room 4? May the Lord have mercy.'

The very mention of the ominous room brought people out into a sweat. Prisoners would cross themselves as they passed it. Guards hated to go near it.

'People go there to die', was the explanation.

Richard tried to eat his gruel but could not. Someone tried to feed him with a spoon, but he was too weak even to swallow. What little food he did manage to get down didn't stay down for long.

Dr. Aldea came and sat down at the side of Richard's bed.

'Friend, I am sorry, but they insist. You'll have to go to Room 4.'

Room 4

The body was barely breathing. It lay there cold and still, the pale spark of life fading slowly, so slowly. Feverish and sweating, the prisoner's clammy skin was wet to the touch. The pallid sickly colour of his skin blended in with the surroundings. The prisoner fitted in, this room was where he was meant to be.

Each breath grates his windpipe and rubs his lungs as if it were sandpaper. Unconscious, the long body of the pastor lies stretched out on the plank. A thin rag covering flapping about in the breeze. The frail grizzled hand of another inmate reaches over to cover him up again. The night moves on. The moon glides out from behind a cloud. The prisoner groans weakly. Hands cross themselves as fellow sufferers look on, helpless. Another night for many spent in captivity – only this is Room 4. People die here.

'Will he make it through tonight, do you think?'

A muffled voice replied in the darkness. 'Who, Wurmbrand? Shouldn't think so. Alexi, look at him – he's worse than last night. We didn't think he'd make it through that, did we?'

'No, but he did. He pulled through in the end. Maybe he'll make it through tonight too. Sergei – you should be more positive. He would have us pray for him. Should we pray?'

Looking over at his cell-mate, Sergei appeared puzzled at this sudden interest in religion. 'Do you want to?'

'Do you?'

'Oh, very well then.'

'Should we kneel?'

'No, my knees won't take it. God is just going to have to listen to us, knees or no knees.'

Quietly two heads bowed and two hearts pleaded for the life of the 'pastor'. A vigil was kept throughout the night, interrupted only by quiet groans from the far-off bed.

The night moved on, blessed relief for some, endless silent agony for others.

'Sergei. Psssttt. Sergei.'

'What is it this time Alexi? Why won't you just leave me alone and go to sleep?'

'Sergei. Lean over and see if he's still alive.'

'Oh all right.' Sergei placed a cold hand over the pastor's heart. 'Yes, just.'

'Tuck his blanket in a bit better then. Does he need any water?'

'Maybe just a touch. Don't move Alexi, let me get it. With your legs he'd be waiting till morning for water.'

Sergei shuffled over to the pail of water in the corner. Taking a ladle he shuffled back, careful not to spill any.

'Here, sip on this. Yes, just a little, that's right. There, no more? Go to sleep then. God bless you pastor. Sleep well.'

Pausing to check that the blanket was tucked in, Sergei sighed.

'Poor chap. He'll not be with us long. That's what I think. Dr. Aldea will have to see him in the morning... Now Alexi – go to sleep!'

The early morning sun rose up over the prison wall.

Birds began to sing. The pastor hung on. The inmates of Room 4 woke up from a broken sleep.

'Is the pastor still with us? Does he look any better?'

'He's still with us. Praise the Lord.'

Richard's very presence in Room 4 awoke something in the lives of the other prisoners. A sense of the spiritual, a knowledge of God, an atmosphere of brotherly love. In the room where every prisoner was at death's door – every prisoner looked on anxiously. Every prisoner was pleading with someone they didn't know for the life of a stranger.

Then the doctor walked in.

'How is he?'

Dr. Aldea bent lovingly over the tall frame of Richard Wurmbrand, his friend.

'No better I see. If only I had better drugs. Some Streptomycin would help ... if only...'

Two weeks passed, four prisoners died.

'Sergei. It's been a fortnight. Four of the others have died but he still hangs on.'

'Yes, Alexi, old friend,' Sergei's eyes twinkle mischievously, 'our prayers must be working? What do you think?'

'Yes, that must be it. Answered prayer.' Alexi smiled a big broad smile.

Sergei stared at his suddenly joyful friend and felt really strange. All this love, this kindness to others, it was a new feeling – a strange one. Huffing and puffing Sergei tried to ignore this new emotion and dismiss it as some new form of insanity. 'Alexi you're going mad – grinning like a chimp all the time! Quit smiling so much and go back to your bed. Lie down, you'll make yourself ill.' Sniggering at his own joke, Sergei laughed out loud, 'Make yourself ill. Huh, how ridiculous... What are we if we're not ill?'

But then something happened. Richard's eyes slowly opened, but only for a few seconds. The fever closed his eyes again and oblivion set in. Once more the other prisoners, the old bench beds, the rags, the smell, the dirt all fell gradually out of focus. Blurry vision, foggy faces, far-off voices – then out! Richard fell back into the world that he had just come from.

The other prisoners gasped, astonished.

'I think he opened his eyes just then? Did you see it?'

'I, well, I don't know, something happened – Is he still breathing?'

'I'll check.... Yes he is, he's still with us.'

'He's still hanging on! You know, he might make it yet. He might just make it!'

'Someone call the Doctor, quick!'

A quick examination was all that Aldea needed. Turning to the rest of Room 4 he smiled broadly. 'I think this pastor is going to live.'

Faces all round the room broke into smiles.

'The pastor is going to live. The pastor is going to live!'

'The Doctor says he's going to live. Did you hear that? Isn't that amazing? Room 4 has a survivor!'

'He's all right, he is over the worst. The doctor said so, did you hear? The pastor is going to live!'

Sergei turned to Alexi and winked.

'The pastor is back with us Alexi —now you're really going to have to behave!'

Alexi just sat back and grinned!

* * *

A few hours passed and Richard's fever left him. The sweat wiped off his forehead he opened his eyes again and took a good long look around.

'Twelve beds quite close together. The windows are open, I can just see out of this one beside me – oh, there are men over there digging in a vegetable patch. Beyond that some barbed wire and a high wall.'

Richard took another quick survey of the room and its surroundings.

'There doesn't seem to be any warders around here. Why would that be? Umm – could be because of the TB – they won't want to get infected. Well that's good – more peace and quiet for me.'

Alexi moved to the edge of his bed and smiled at Richard.

'Pastor, it is great to see you back with us. My name is Alexi.'

Richard smiled back and murmured faintly.

'My name is Richard. I do not see prison guards – quite quiet.'

'Yes, it has its advantages this TB. It certainly means that this prison is one of the less rigorous prisons around.' Alexi took a miniscule rag and gently wiped Richard's forehead. 'However, we get virtually nothing in the way of supplies. Basic food rations and that's about it. Whatever you find in the way of clothing, material, fabric – keep a hold of it. You'll need it sooner or later to patch up all the holes. I've got a big hole just here and it is letting in the drafts something awful!'

Alexi pointed at a great big tear near the top of his trouser leg. It seemed as if his clothes hung onto him by a thread!

Other prisoners started to mill around Richard's bed curious to see the pastor who had just about come back from the dead.

'Are you really a pastor?'

'Yes, that is why I am here. I love God. A capital offence these days.' Richard coughed again. His fever had left him but the cough still hounded him.

A bitter voice broke in from across the room.

'I totally believe all Marxist teachings about religion! The Church is just another oppressor of us poor workers.'

Alexi whispered in Richard's ear, 'That's Filipescu – not a religious man.'

Richard turned to where the voice was coming from. Filip was carrying on full throttle.

'All you ministers are just out for what you can get from the rich and you tell the poor not to worry about all the hardship and poverty and injustice today – cos they're going to get their reward tomorrow. What rubbish!!'

Filip was only stopped by a massive fit of coughing. Blood was staining the man's fingers and he was hot and feverish.

Over the next few weeks Richard spoke gently with him, but Filip's energy was fading fast as the TB got a stronger and stronger hold of him.

Richard woke up one evening to find Alexi shaking him on the shoulder.

'Richard, wake up Richard, Filip is calling for you. It won't be long now. The illness has got too great a hold on him.'

Sergei muttered something about the decrepit old pastor never managing it to the end of his bed far less across the room. After a bit of persuasion by Alexi,

Richard was carried by Sergei over to Filip's bed.

Filip looked up into the eyes of his two fellow-prisoners.

'I love Jesus,' he said. Then he died.

The following morning the inmates watched out the window as Filipescu was thrown into a mass grave along with the many other prisoners who had also died that week.

Richard sat and spoke to a couple of the others.

'A man calls himself an atheist[1] as he sits with his wife over tea and cakes. He can say, "I don't believe in God" when his life is going well and he has no problems. That is no proof of atheism. A true conviction must survive enormous pressure, and atheism does not. Atheism does not survive the pressure of death and eternity. When death is near, the man who doesn't believe in God suddenly finds himself face to face with God.'

* * *

An expectant whisper sounded out from one of the prisoners.

'Gafencu's friend has just smuggled something in.'

Excited eyes stared over to Valeriu Gafencu.

'What is it Val, show us what you have?'

Sitting on the edge of his bed, his hands untied a piece of twisted paper, unwrapping something inside.

'Why, it is sugar!'

Sugar. Sweetness. Pure concentrated, refined energy. Everyone longed for the sweetness on their tongue. The wasted bodies craved it. What a prize. All the eyes of Room 4 followed every movement of the crystal white cubes. Quietly they were put aside as Val turned to the

1. Atheism - see page 19.

friend who brought it.

'Thank you, but I shall not eat it now. Someone might need it more than me. I will save it for them.'

With that he placed it in a safe place and turned to say goodbye to his friend.

'What a fortunate chap, a visitor and a piece of sugar. But decent of him not to eat it like that. Very decent.'

All of Room 4 agreed that it was a very generous act.

A few days later Richard's fever increased again. Hot and sweaty he lay on his bed exhausted and dehydrated. Gafencu passed the sugar-lump to his neighbour who passed it to his neighbour and round the room the sugar-lumps came until it finally stopped on Richard's pillow.

'It is a gift,' whispered Gafencu.

'Thank you – but I shall not take it now – someone else may have need ...' and the sugar-lumps went on, and on, and on...

Room Four held on and fought through. They knew if they didn't hold each other up they would all fall. Any hope was to be grasped and snatched back from the world of grey walls and iron bars. Keep going, keep going, keep going, keep going ... just keep going – and – the sugar lumps kept going ... and going ... and going ... for two whole years.

***

But it was not always peaceful. Tempers flared, tension mounted – in some more than others – Sergeant Bucar for one. He had fallen foul of the Communist party and was in jail as a result. For some tortured, twisted reason he took pride and sick enjoyment out of telling his fellow-prisoners the gory details of his past exploits. He would go on and on about how he hated Jews, how he liked to beat them up, how he just could not stand them. The others in Room 4 just could not stand him.

Faces would turn the other way, eyes would look in another direction, disgust pale across already white cheek-bones. 'This is how you do it,' – and as if reciting a recipe he would rattle through his 101 ways of beating the stuffing out of Jews, subordinates and criminals – in that order.

Dr. Aldea however was worried about him – Bucar was dying – but doing a very good job of ignoring the fact.

'Dr. Aldea,' he whined, 'why do you insist in keeping me here when it is obvious that there is nothing wrong with me – have the men grown so attached to me and my razor-wit that you can't bear to separate them from me?' Bucar laughed at his own joke, coughing up blood with the effort. 'Look at me – I'm not like the others!'

'No,' Aldea snapped, 'You're much worse! Stop arguing with me and start thinking about your soul!'

'Who do you think you are?' Bucar screamed at the retreating back of Dr. Aldea. 'Jewish blood – that's Aldea's problem – I can spot the filthy JEWISH blood a mile off!'

Bucar's coughing got worse, his health deteriorating as rapidly as his peace of mind. His cock-sure bravado, his calm assurance, his selfish pride – crumbled as wet sand crumbles between your fingers. Bucar found himself floundering.

'Why me?' he asked softly one night. 'I don't want to die! Why me?' Richard turned over in his bed and whispered across the backs of sleeping prisoners to the desperation sounding out from the far corner of the room.

'You feel now you have no reason to hope – but the night is darkest before sunrise. Christians believe that dawn will come. "God may kill me, but still I will trust in him." Have faith in the darkest moment.'

Turning his back to Richard, Bucar lay quietly – then slept. For hours the next day Bucar was unconscious – Dr. Aldea regularly checked his progress. Clenched lips and anxious eyes gave away the desperate situation. Room 4 waited for another exit. Bucar awoke troubled, something weighing down on him, a burden too heavy for him to hold.

'I want to confess before you all – I have sinned so much.' Breathing was even more difficult for him as he sobbed out the pain and horror that had threatened to drag him down. Many, many Jews had been killed by his hand, a woman, a boy of twelve. Women had held their babies and children in their arms – until Bucur had snatched them away – killing the babes sometimes still in their mother's arms. Desperate screams, sobbing, children's tears and cries all came back to haunt him. Children's arms grasping, clutching – then soft and limp.

'Richard – you will hate me now.'

'No – it is you who hate. You hate this creature who used to kill, you have rejected this man. You are no longer a murderer. A man can be born again.'

The following morning his story finally ended, – a hoarse rattle sounded from within his throat. His pale tortured hands clasped the small rusty crucifix then relaxed. He had gone. In death his face showed a peace that he had never known in life.

***

Richard sat hunched over at the end of his bed. Another last-minute rescue. Another man ushered into heaven by the skin of his teeth.

'Why did he confess all these things – just at the last minute – why did he do that?'

Richard rose slightly and looked at the faces of the men gathered round the miracle of bones and tissue that was once Sergeant Bucar. Richard let his thoughts speak, 'Why did he confess? ... Once I lived near a railway. I never noticed the trains by day because the town was noisy. But at night I heard their whistles clearly. The clamour of life can deafen us to the quiet voice of our conscience. It is when death approaches in the silence of the prison, where there are no distractions, that men hear the voice of God, who never have before...' Richard's voice trailed off into the silence.

***

Professor Popp was one of Richard's special pals. This morning he stood over Richard with a rough hessian cloth desperately searching for a very dirty bar of old soap that had somehow got lost in all the excitement of finding the thing in the first place.

'Hmmm, I just find the thing and then it slips out of my grasp!' he muttered feeling around for the soap underneath the wooden bench. 'If I can ever get a hand on this soap, Pastor Wurmbrand, I will give you a very good scrub with it but ... bother ... come back here ... it's dirty and probably no use at all but it is soap and all we have and I am not going to lose it under this bed ... ah ha! Got you!!' Professor Popp stood up straight, grinning from ear to ear, and set to. Richard was not strong enough to wash himself and relied continuously on the kindness of Popp. As gently as Popp could he would scrub him with the rough cloth and a little bit of soap if it was around.

Popp chuckled to himself.

'Of course being a Communist prison we have all the modern conveniences of the 20th century. Why, down the corridor there are a full set of showers – however, none of them work!' Popp chuckled again and a warm wrinkly smile spread over his whole face. Smiles were like treasure here. Richard loved to see his friend smile.

'In the Bible,' Richard remembered out loud, 'it says that God laughs. In the second psalm I think.'

Popp looked at Richard incredulously.

'Laughs? God laughs?' he said trying to picture this new and amazing fact. Popp washed Richard's tired pale face and sighed.

'There's not much that God could find to laugh about here.' Popp's smile faded. Richard didn't like to see Popp's eyes loose their sparkle. 'Where is God, Pastor, why doesn't he help us?'

'Popp, let me tell you a story.'

'Oh good. The pastor is going to tell us a story – shhh.'

Ears pricked up around Room 4 as Richard lay back. Popp took the cloth, gave Richard a quick dry behind the ears, and sat down.

'There was a pastor called to a man's deathbed. He walked into the kitchen and found the huddled shape of the youngest daughter sobbing her heart out as her mother bent over her child and tried to comfort her. The young girl turned when she heard the pastor and said, "Where is this protecting arm of God you preach about pastor?"

He stood and stared at the scene before him.

'Child – it is on your shoulder in the shape of your mother's arm.'

'So, Popp, Christ is with us in many ways. Firstly he can be seen in the Christian doctors who are beaten and bullied but continue to help us. Some doctors have been jailed for trying to help us. There are priests and pastors here in prison who try to ease our burdens, other Christians come to give us food and clothes. Then there are still others who teach us about God. But remember that God is also with you when you yourself serve others. "Whenever you did this for one of the least important of these brothers of mine, you did it for me!"'

Popp turned back to scrubbing Richard's back. 'How is it that Richard always seems to know what to say?'

***

'Richard look ... outside ... a whole bunch of newcomers. Some look worse than us – we'll have to make more room to fit them in ... now how are we going to do that?' Alexi grumbled he was already sharing his bench with another prisoner so further occupants were not welcome.

Alexi however had no say in the matter and new occupants arrived in Room 4. One gentleman in particular attracted a lot of attention – Boris Matei.

As sick as the rest of them in Room 4 he insisted on harping on about the 'caring Communist', 'the wonderful Communist party', 'all my great Communist friends'. On and on and on he rumbled. 'The Communists are the conquerors of the world! Communism will go on for ever!' He never stopped.

'It's incredible really, doesn't he know who put him

116

in here?'

'I think he thinks that the authorities will soon realise what an awful mistake they have made and welcome him back with open arms ... poor fool.'

Richard and Boris had long discussions regarding Communism, faith, and belief but Boris was unreachable and very, very stubborn.

'Not even a fifteen-year sentence has cured him of Communism – my arguments are not getting anywhere.'

Richard looked at the ardent Communist. 'I'll have to be careful of him. He might be an informer. But even if he is I am still going to speak my mind. Now that I am in prison, suffering from TB, being tortured and beaten there is nothing more they can do to me. I have more free speech behind these four walls than throughout the whole of Romania.'

Re-education

Popp and Alexi sat on either side of Richard's bed. Alexi looked tense, Popp looked worried. They were in the middle of discussing some rather frightening news.

' ... the old priest in Room 7 said that there was definitely something up ... I guess they must have overheard one of the guards talking about it.' Alexi scratched himself vigorously on the thigh, 'Oh, these fleas are really bothering me today!'

'Hmmm.' Popp pondered. 'What is this Re-education anyway? Going back to school? I wouldn't mind going back to school.'

'No! I told you - Popp- it's much more sinister than that ... the Communists aren't about to give us any favours...'

Sergei bent over from the next bed and put in his opinion.

'I heard that in the Piteshi and Suceava jails the Re-education was with beatings and not with books.'

Alexi looked tense. Popp looked worried. Sergei wished he hadn't said anything. Richard prayed.

Boris ... laughed.

'You don't believe all that gossip do you? I know these men better than you and they won't do that. Many of these men are old colleagues of mine – we drank a beer together, had a smoke, discussed politics, our wives drank coffee together and went shopping,' he chuckled. 'I can't believe you all fall for the tiniest piece of gossip that comes your way ... you'll see ... there's nothing in it. What idiots you all are ... thank Lenin there is one person here who can see sense!'

'Hmmm,' Popp muttered to himself. 'We shall soon see, no doubt.'

He wasn't wrong. Within a week news spread through the prison like wild-fire. The leader of the Re-education committee had arrived and had instructions to begin at once.

What soon started was to completely change the atmosphere of the prison.

'Richard!' Alexi coughed up blood, and tried to stand up. 'Richard!'

'Stay there Alexi, don't move.' Richard tried to move closer to his injured friend. But he was still too weak even to get out of his own bed. 'It's like a wave of madness has come over this whole place ... shh, now lie still, that leg mustn't be moved. Where is Dr. Aldea?'

That morning the prison authorities had implemented the new scheme. Every 50 prisoners had an extra 10 prisoners added to their numbers. These ten prisoners were all hand picked for their Communist leanings and gifts of brutality. Alexi had been set upon by one of these hand-picked prisoners this morning. It was late in the afternoon and still Dr. Aldea had not appeared.

'... Richard ... why? why me? Why did they do that?' Alexi lay back on the wooden bench, his pallid complexion in stark contrast to the blood smeared all over this face. 'All these people watching – entertainment for them...'

'It is this system, Alexi. If they beat us hard enough and often enough they think they will get us to give in and side with the Communists. Lie back now, the doctor should be here soon.' Richard looked anxiously to the door to check for any sign of Dr. Aldea, but there was none.' These new prisoners are out to gain points, the more of us they break the more points they get.' Richard furtively checked out who was in the room.

'No one to worry about.' Richard thought. All the new recruits were off looking for other prisoners to trap.

Alexi's eyes were moist with tears. Hatred and suffering ruled within the prison walls.

Richard was glad he had not seen it happen. The marks on Alexi's body showed where a mallet and chain had been brought down crushing his fragile body.

'Alexi, these men are cruel but they are being tricked as well. Someone has deceived them into thinking that if they beat us they will win their freedom. They deceive others too.'

'Boris.' Alexi's face scrunched up. 'Boris was an idiot to do what he did ... but they didn't need to do that to him. That was awful.'

Richard's mind wandered back to that morning. It had been awful. Many of the fitter prisoners had been instructed to stand outside in the cold to welcome some official visitors. Guards came over and created a barrier between the prisoners and the main thoroughfare into the prison.

Sergei, on form as usual with all the latest news, tried to attract Alexi's attention.

'Psst ... The latest news hot off the press – do you want to hear it?'

Alexi leant closer and Sergei continued.

'We're expecting visitors today.'

120

'Yes? Who?'

'Well, that's it – there could be a problem – they're something to do with Re-education.'

'That word makes a man sick with fear.' Alexi turned towards the sound of the creaking gates.

Sergei stiffened again and muttered to himself.

'Well, here goes.'

The big gates opened to their left and a group of well dressed government officials exited out of a selection of government-type vehicles. Re-education specialists on their rounds, checking on the progress of the new scheme. They were accompanied by leaders of the party, government ministers and high-ranking civil servants. Boris strained his neck to see what was going on. Sergei turned on Boris with a scornful scowl. He began to mimic Boris in a squeaky voice.

'I know these men, I've had a drink with them, discussed politics, our wives have shopped together – BAH! Rubbish! Little man, stop squirming – accept it, these men are brutes – Re-education is here to stay. Don't fool yourself any more!'

Boris desperately tried to hang on to the last shred of hope he had in his party. He desperately wanted to believe in these men. They were, after all, all he had left. Straining to see over the heads of Sergei and Alexi, Boris's eyes sparkled in recognition.

'We shall see, Sergei, we shall see. Jianu, my friend, Jianu.' Boris shoved past the crowds. Sergei, panicking, reached out to grab Boris back. 'What does he think he's doing? Get back here you old fool...'

Boris, out of reach of his fellow prisoners continued across the court yard to Jianu.

'Who is this Jianu anyway?' muttered Alexi.

'He must be one of the grey suits. An old Communist buddy.' Sergei made a move as if to go after Boris.

'Don't worry Sergei.' Alexi grabbed Sergei by the wrist. 'The guards will stop him.' A thick line of guards stood between Boris and the official visitors. One guard pushed him, another grabbed him from behind and began to drag him back to the prisoners.

One of the Re-educated prisoners, a hand-picked bully, came out of a side door and walked towards an area in front of the visitors. A voice ordered the man to go ahead with the demonstration. The honoured guests looked on. A guard moved towards the prisoners scanning them, looking over them, deciding. Starting at one end of the line he walked past prisoner after prisoner, his eyes stopped at Sergei but then he turned and let his eyes rest on Alexi. Alexi knew what was going to happen. Sergei could see the panic in Alexi's eyes.

'Leave him – don't touch him.' Sergei pushed himself in-between the guard and Alexi, but a quick fist in his face flung Sergei to the ground grovelling in the dirt. Alexi screamed as he was dragged towards the frantic crowd. The grey suits were getting excited, the hands that held the chain and mallet were tensing – ready for action. A mallet came crashing down, Alexi ducked and weaved but was caught on the back with a heavy iron chain. Grey suits and polished shoes looked on. Notebooks and diaries were scribbled in. Discussion and debate abounded concerning this amazing new system. Alexi lay bleeding in the dirt.

'Congratulations gentlemen on providing this entertainment for us ... prisoners beating other prisoners.

This is an inspired idea.' Jianu smiled, obviously enjoying the spectacle. The smile faded. A scruffy, dishevelled old man was running and shouting at him from across the courtyard.

Boris had got through the guards.

'Jianu, friend, comrade – stop please. Don't allow this to go on – please.'

Alexi's eyes flickered. A voice from his left shouted, 'Beat him again man, he's not quite finished yet.' The chain and mallet came down once more.

Jianu ignored Boris, but rose to address the shocked prisoners and the excited onlookers. He pointed one fat chubby fist towards the grovelling Boris. 'Take this man away – he is in need of some Re-education!'

Sergei groaned. There was nothing any of them could do.

Alexi was left lying in the dirt. Boris was set upon with the mallet and chain.

* * *

'There was nothing anybody could do,' sighed Richard.

Alexi looked questioningly at Richard. 'Boris?' he whispered.

'Boris gave in. He's one of them now. The last Sergei saw was Boris grovelling in the dirt, kissing the hands of the torturers, thanking them for showing him the error of his ways, for showing him the light.'

Alexi screwed up his face in disgust. 'Even now, even after that, he doesn't see the lies, the evil, the deceit.'

Richard sighed. 'Some of the men are injured in their minds as well as their bodies. They will do and say anything to avoid further beatings. Boris didn't want to give up on Communism. Communism is his life even though Communists tried to kill him.'

The evening sun sank quickly behind the skyline as Alexi lay back and tried to rest. Richard looked on unable to do anything for his injured friend. 'I am worried about the doctor. It's evening now. I haven't seen him all day.'

The morbid peace of the prison cells was suddenly shattered by further screams. More beatings, more Re-education. A small crowd of prisoners rushed to the door as they tried to decipher who the screams belonged to. Richard still bed-ridden could not make out who it was.

Sergei was amongst the first at the door. His face was pale. He recognised two different voices. Richard turned towards his friend.

'What is it Sergei? What's happening?'

'It's Boris – he's beating Dr. Aldea. Aldea's been caught!'

* * *

The moon shone serenely through the iron bars. If you shut your ears and looked beyond the metal rods you could almost kid yourself you were somewhere peaceful, serene, a haven. All you had to do, however, was take your fingers out of your ears and reality struck home. Screams haunted the midnight hours, the serenity of the moon seemed to be a cruel joke laughing at you through the iron bars, laughing, laughing, laughing until the morning.

The prisoners lay there trying to hide from the screams. Richard leaned over the edge of his bed – he felt sick.

* * *

The news that came the following morning was that Aldea had been found a bed in Room 4. Laying down on the hard wooden bench was excruciatingly painful for him as Boris's whip had lashed across Aldea's back, scraping the flesh away, cutting through boils, opening up old wounds. Aldea lay there sweating and shivering in turn. That afternoon the cell door opened and a man stood at the foot of Dr. Aldea's bed.

'There is a prisoner seriously ill and he is asking for you.'

Alexi, whispered hoarsely, 'The doctor is far too ill to move.'

Aldea turned and asked quietly, 'Who is it?'

Sheepishly the messenger muttered, 'It's Boris.'

Aldea climbed painfully out of his bed. Nobody spoke as he stumbled from the room.

* * *

'Look, someone smashes a window as a signal, then we start.'

'Start what?'

'Breaking windows, shouting, screaming, all sorts of bedlam. We'll be heard – no doubt about it – the football stadium is just across the road. The whole town will be there at 5 pm precisely.'

Plans were afoot to create a disturbance, to bring to the town's attention the fate of the prisoners, tortured underneath their very noses.

Alexi turned to Richard.

'Should Christians do this? What about turning the other cheek?' Alexi wasn't sure.

Richard was in no doubt.

'Jesus is usually portrayed as 'meek and mild' – but he was a fighter too. He drove the merchants from the temple with a whip.'

Others joined in the debate.

'Yes, he called the Pharisees vipers and snakes – there's nothing gentle about that.'

When the time came for the football match, excitement mounted in the prison. At 5 pm precisely the signal was given – a window pane was shattered and the revolt began. Windows were broken, plates and mugs cracked open, chairs smashed and a steady chant went up – 'Help us! Help us! Help us!'

The football game ground to a halt and the whole town gathered outside the prison walls. Guards lashed out at the prisoners with clubs beating them back, trampling them under their feet. Boris was one of the prisoners crushed in the mad rush to escape the clubs of the advancing guards.

The anxious onlookers were swept away by guards brandishing rifles.

The revolt was crushed and the ringleaders punished. Some were taken to a prison where no medical care was given. They died as a result.

Once again Dr. Aldea went to sit beside Boris's bed. He nursed him and cared for him, until Boris too was moved to another jail. Only then did Aldea rejoin the inmates in Room 4.

'Boris was moved this morning,' he muttered

Room 4 looked at Dr. Aldea. Here he was, still bearing the scars and wounds from Boris's beating. He had cared for Boris, loved him even, forgiven him totally. Perhaps they were imagining it but he even sounded sad that Boris had left. Richard smiled in admiration – 'He is living the life of Christ. These men can see Christ when they look at him.'

Richard closed his eyes and opened his heart in prayer to his Father in heaven. 'Even in sadness and sorrow, some mornings it is just so good to be alive. Thank you, God, for your people whose lives are lives that show you. The people look at them and they look at you.' The old Abbott was just like that...

'Can we do anything for him?' Sergei had asked one night.

'No,' Dr. Aldea turned and walked away. 'Let him die in peace.'

'What about the other prisoner?'

Aldea looked at Valiescu who lay doubled up in pain. 'Watch him, he may die tonight too.'

'Both of them?' asked one of the prisoners. 'How strange if they were to die together!'

'Why is it strange?' asked Sergei.

'The Abbot was tortured at the canal labour camp – it is the worst camp by far – anyway, this young man was one of the prisoners hired to be a taskmaster by the authorities. Vasilescu was in charge of a group of priests. Old Abbot Iscu would have been whipped by a young man like this, and now they are both lying in the same ward, both about to die.'

That night, Richard remembered how the young man had reached over and whispered urgently in his ear.

'Pastor, pray for me. I am going.' Then the silence was broken by his tortured cry, 'I believe in God.' He began to weep.

Almost immediately another voice came from

127

Richard's other side.

'Lift me up, take me to him.'

Voices came from all over Room 4.

'Don't do it Iscu, you're too ill, let us go to him.'

'No!' he said. 'I must! Lift me out!'

A few prisoners, under direct orders, lifted the weak, frail, priest over to Vasilescu's bed. A beautiful smile spread over Iscu's face.

The tortured smiled at the torturer and said soothingly, 'You are young, you hardly knew what you were doing.' He wiped sweat off the young man's brow. 'I forgive you with all my heart, and so would other Christians too. If we forgive, surely Christ, who is better than us, will forgive you too. There is a place in heaven for you also.' Vasilescu and the Abbot shared communion together before Abbot Iscu was carried off to his own bed.

That night they both died.

Richard lay back and thought, 'maybe they went to heaven together, hand in hand.'

* * *

Winter came with a vengeance. December was a cold, cold month, one of the coldest on record. Men went from day to day shivering, eking out a living from the scraps flung at them. Rotten carrot soup got thinner and thinner as the year drew to a close. Room 4 got busier and busier as the cold and hunger claimed more victims. Then Christmas came.

'I can't believe it's Christmas today.' Alexi looked longingly out the window at the snow shining in the moonlight.

'Merry Christmas then,' grunted Sergei '... and a happy New Year while we're at it!'

'Hmmm,' Popp muttered, 'Merry Christmas indeed.' Popp had lost his sparkle. Before the Re-education had started he had been moved to another prison, only to be moved back to Tirgul Ocna the day before. 'Merry Christmas for some, I suppose,' he went on.

'Cheer up Popp.' Alexi was determined to get a smile out of him once more. 'Smile for me.'

'Smile! Smile?' Popp stared at Alexi, 'I have been to a prison where an Orthodox priest committed suicide rather than betray his faith. Others threw themselves out of windows, one man starved himself and nobody noticed!'

Popp shrunk into himself, staring at the ground beneath his feet.

From deep within the prison, somewhere down in the dark depths of corridors and cells a voice rose up from the dirt, reaching for the heavens. At first still and quiet the voice gradually swelled wonderfully in the crisp clear air. It echoed through the corridors and everybody turned to listen. Even the guards stopped to listen to the song, a haunting melody. Nobody said a word, they froze, not wanting to move – afraid to break the beauty.

Silence came once more. Richard sat up in his bed and in a hushed whispered voice he told them about another song.

'... the song of Christ is the song we must all sing. When the Messiah comes many will try and sing their own songs, and their tunes will be harsh. We must sing Jesus' song, the song of His life, passions, joys, sufferings, death and resurrection. Only then will the music be true. It is a song like that which we have just heard, this Christmas in the jail of Tirgul Ocna.'

***

Winter came and went but the cold always seemed to hang around the prison.

Richard rubbed his arms and feet. 'Brrrr, it is so cold, even though the sun shines outside I feel like ice in here.'

'We all do,' Popp was stamping his feet to get warm.

Dr. Aldea backed in through the door at Room 4 giving directions like, 'Take care, watch the corner, gently now.'

Everybody sat up and stared as a man with his back completely encased in a plaster cast was manoeuvred into position. The guards left him and immediately he stretched his arm into a gap in his plaster. Richard gasped as he saw pages being turned, and printed words and paper. 'It's a book,' exclaimed Richard! No prisoner in the whole jail had access to anything like this!

Richard looked at the book – 'Is it, could it be?' Before Richard could ask, the man turned to him and said, 'It's the Gospel of John, would you like to borrow it?'

Richard reached eagerly. Gently he held it in his hands. This was like gold dust, but more valuable, better than a drug that could save his life. Richard read it from cover to cover then had to pass it on to the next man who did the same. It was hard to give it up but over the next few months many read the gospel and learnt it by heart. Popp read it too. He had lived amongst Christians for so long now and was keen to find out exactly what was behind the whole thing. Popp talked long into the night about what he was reading in the gospel but his last barrier to faith was how he should pray to Jesus.

Richard cleared his throat and everyone knew that that was the signal for another story.

'...There was a pastor who was called to an old man's deathbed. He went to sit in an armchair close to the bed, but the old man said, "Please don't sit there!" So the pastor pulled up a stool and the old man began to explain the story of the armchair.

"Fifty years ago, when I was a lad, an old pastor asked if I said my prayers. I replied, 'No, I have no-one to pray to. If I shout at the top of my voice the man on the floor above does not hear me so how will God who is all that way up there in heaven?'

The old pastor said mildly, 'Do not try to pray then, just sit quietly and look at that chair. Imagine that Jesus is sitting there as he sat before in so many homes in Palestine. What would you tell him?' Young, and fool-hardy I said, 'If I were honest, I'd say that I didn't believe in him!' 'Well,' said the pastor, 'that shows at least what is really on your mind. You could go further and challenge him to prove that he exists. If you don't like the way he is doing things, tell him – David and Job did the same. If you want something, ask him for it. If you get it, say thank you. That is prayer. Don't recite holy phrases! Say what is really in your heart.'

The old dying man went on. 'I didn't believe in Christ, but I did in the old pastor. To please him I went ahead and pretended Christ was in that armchair. For a few days it was a game and then I knew that he was with me. I spoke to a real Jesus about real things. Prayer became a conversation. So, young man, fifty years have passed and every day I speak with Jesus in that chair.'

With that the old man died, his arm stretched out in love towards his invisible Christ sitting in his armchair...'

Professor Popp looked into the blue eyes of his friend. 'Richard, when I first saw you I had this feeling that you had something to give me. Jesus is real to me. Thank you dear friend.'

As the prisoners turned to chat about another of Wurmbrand's stories an excited voice came from a cell down the corridor.

'Hey! Hey! You chaps in Room 4 listen up!'

Sergei shouted down the corridor, 'Yes, what is it?'

'Stalin is dead!' the voice replied.

'Stalin is dead?' Sergei couldn't believe it.

'Stalin, the Russian Communist Dictator – that Stalin?'

'What other Stalin is there? He is dead!'

Whoops of joy and celebrations broke out all over the prison. Guards cursed and walked about nervously. Things were bound to change. The political upheaval in Russia would spread to Romania. 'Maybe things will change for us,' whispered Popp.

And they did ... the old regime was thrown over. Some government officials in charge of Re-education were executed, others imprisoned, Re-education was scrapped and the whole sordid situation calmed down.

***

Excitement mounted about the death of Stalin and it was the only topic of conversation when Dr. Aldea came into Room 4 to do his rounds.

Aldea stopped his examination of Richard and looked

132

at him, a puzzled expression across his face. Taking up his stethoscope again he continued his examination. Shaking his head he smiled and laughed, long and loud.

'We can't make you out. Your lungs are like a sieve, your spine's affected too. I haven't been able to give you treatment of any kind but you're not getting any worse. In fact, as you know, you have been able to walk this week – the first time in months. Richard, you are getting better, you are now going to leave Room 4.'

Shouts and whistles went up, those who could stand stood and waved their hands in the air, others made as much noise as they could from their bedsides.

'How's it done pastor?' joked Sergei. 'Why doesn't that old body of yours obey orders and die?'

Richard smiled round at all his friends, Popp, Sergei, Alexi, and Dr. Aldea. He cleared his throat and for the last time in Room 4 they all listened to the old Lutheran pastor. He was short and to the point.

'It is a miracle and an answer to prayer!'

With that Richard was escorted from Room 4, the first to leave alive after two and a half years.

Alexi and Sergei looked at each other and smiled.

'Do you remember?' Alexi murmured.

'Yes, that first night he came. I was shuffling around getting the water, checking on him every five minutes. You couldn't move because of your legs ... you asked if we should pray ... yes, I remember that.'

'He said his healing was an answer to prayer and we prayed that first night, way back then.' Alexi remembered the fervent prayers from both of them, the anxious all-night vigil for a pastor that neither of them knew.

Sergei stared round the rest of Room 4. 'Lots of us

prayed, I remember. Maybe Richard will never know exactly how many people have been praying for him. There's been you and me, hundreds of others who met him behind these walls, maybe thousands outside this prison, even outside this country. There'll be a big get together of us in heaven that's for sure – Hey, it will be fun.'

Alexi looked a bit shocked at the flippancy, but smiled. Sergei sounded as if he might yet become a believer. Taking a deep breath Alexi realised God still had a job to do in Room 4 even though Richard wasn't there any more.

New Cell, Old Problems

'Pass that ladle to me, I'm next,' the sharp quarrelsome tone harped on at Richard who was taking his daily ration of water from the tub. The bitter twisted face glared at this new prisoner. 'Another pastor is something, frankly, I could do without!'

Richard quickly moved away to find a corner to escape to. That was hard in such cramped conditions. Richard squashed into a corner at the back of the room and gazed at his new world over the edge of his cup.

'I'd forgotten how petty and nasty this other world could be. Room 4 had an atmosphere of death but it meant that the men knew what was important. They left all this play-acting at life behind. It was real, it was a life to be proud of. Huh, there's that old brigadier moaning as usual. Yesterday he refused to talk to me because I forgot to call him Brigadier. I wish my old friends were here. We used to have such talks, even though we were dying. Someone would be in pain but he would still laugh at a joke or smile at a neighbour.'

Richard was generally fed up with these pathetic human specimens, so full of life but dead of soul.

Weeks went on one after the other. The brigadier left and another soldier came to take his place, this time he was a general, but one with a bit of compassion and a lot of common sense. Richard knew he would get on with him.

'This general has his head screwed on.'

General Stravat was a Christian before he was a soldier. He cared for his 'men' and took great interest in their well-being both physically and spiritually. Between them Richard and Stravat made quite a team.

One morning a parcel was delivered to the cell, c/o General Stravat. Excitement mounted as he untied the string and unwrapped the paper, carefully placing them aside for later use. Inside, his wife had placed –

'Sausages! Look at these fat pink sausages.'

'She's packed him a whole ham! Where did she get that? She must have paid an arm and a leg for it.'

'Wow – fruit cake, my wife used to make the best fruit cake in the whole of Romania!'

Then – 'CHOCOLATE!'

Everyone's eyes popped out at the chocolate. Tongues licked lips and eyes looked longingly at the pile of goodies.

Stravat had lived on scraps for eight years but he wrapped up the parcel again and solemnly walked over to where Richard was seated.

'Pastor, would you be so good as to divide this equally amongst the men?'

* * *

Professor Popp and Richard were talking together in the yard during their exercise break. A lot of chat was going around about the collapse of the canal project and how many of the prisoners working there had now been moved on. Popp had been listening intently to this information and then he spoke to Richard, tense and pale.

'Richard, since my return to Tirgul Ocna I have been keeping something from you.'

136

'What is it friend, don't look so worried, you can tell me.'

'It's Sabina, she is in now in prison, and was at one point working at the canal.'

Richard's breath tightened round his chest, he signalled to Popp to carry on.

'She survived, but Richard, only just. She had to eat grass, snakes, dog, anything that moved.'

'Sabina, Oh Lord, my wife. She is so small, how can she survive?'

Richard insisted on hearing everything that Popp had heard on the prison grapevine. By the end of it, Richard was in a dark, sombre mood. Depression started to eat him up.

'Oh God, are you there? Do you listen to me?' But prayer for Richard was impossible! For days Richard spoke to no-one. Popp and others were worried, but no one could reach him. Richard shrank from the world and hid within himself. Then one morning, out in the exercise yard, he found himself looking at a very strange old man. He stood outside the guard's room with his silvery white beard blowing in the wind. His robes fluttering around his ankles.

'What is that old priest doing here?' Richard asked.

Popp smiled, he had some conversation at last. 'He's come here to listen to confession. It is the Roman Catholic and Orthodox prisoners who make use of him.'

Richard looked longingly at the long line of prisoners who queued up to speak to the old priest. Richard felt an aura of holiness about the man, so much so that he had a great compulsion to tell this old man the whole truth. Richard did not believe in confession in the same way that others did but when it came to his turn Richard felt a great burden lifted off him. He shared with the old priest his sense of despair, his dryness of soul, his black moods. Sins that Richard had never told anyone before were laid bare before the old priest. But instead of looking at Richard with contempt he looked at him in love.

As they sat together sharing their joys and sorrows Richard learnt that this old priest had had much pain. His family were either dead, in prison or had turned away from him completely. But he went about spending his days encouraging others.

Instead of, 'Good morning!' he said, 'Rejoice!' then he would add, 'The day you can't smile don't open your shop. It takes seventeen muscles to smile but forty-three to frown!'

As he left he turned to Richard and said, 'Every day you do not rejoice, my son, is a day lost. You will never have that day again!'

Richard had no choice but to rejoice!

* * *

Every month or so Richard was allowed to receive a small parcel from home. Friends and neighbours all contributed with old clothes, food and, in one parcel, 100 grams of streptomycin was smuggled in. The forbidden drug was a life-saver for those who suffered from TB. Richard could have done with it himself but his mind went back to the men he had left behind in Room 4.

'General Stravat, I have 100 grams of streptomycin – who is the most needy case in Room 4 at this moment?'

General Stravat grimaced. 'Sultaniuc,' he said with

distaste. 'A thorough fascist and a brute! He is at death's door though he will not admit it. Richard you're better off taking it yourself ... well, if you insist.'

Stravat was not away for very long. He soon came back still holding the medicine. 'I'm sorry Richard, he wanted to know where the drug had come from. I told him it was from you and he said there was no way he would take anything from someone who was an opponent of Fascism. You just can't do anything with a fanatic like that.'

Richard sat down to think. 'There might be a way round this, you know,' he muttered. 'Let me think.' Richard turned towards a young man who was in the bed next to him. Josif might just be able to pull it off. 'He won't suspect Josif of anything. Well, here goes. Josif, over here son. I've got a job for you to do.'

Josif trundled over, he was a nice enough young man but was open about his dislike of anything religious. 'I hate God,' he said and Richard believed him.

'What is it, Wurmbrand?'

'The old fascist, Sultaniuc, in Room 4 needs this medicine but he won't take it from me.'

Josif looked at the pile of tablets, rather puzzled. 'Don't you need this stuff yourself?'

'Yes, yes,' said Richard, 'but he needs it more. Go on, take it – say it is from that other fascist down the hallway. He is sure to take it then.'

But five minutes later, Josif was back. 'The old goat won't take it. He's certain that no other fascist would ever give him anything and he still suspects that it is from you. The only way he is going to take this is if you swear on oath that it does not come from you.'

Richard smiled and said, 'Why not? This drug doesn't belong to me, it belongs to God!

So Josif trundled back to Room 4 just a little bit bemused. Just then Dr. Aldea came into Richard's cell on his rounds. Bending over he listened to Richard's chest and gave him the once over.

'Hmm. Not bad Richard, but if we ever get hold of some Streptomycin you should take it.'

Richard smiled to himself as Josif thundered back along the corridor.

'Well that's that. He took it at last!'

'Took what?' Dr. Aldea looked suspiciously at Richard. 'What are you two up to?'

'The Streptomycin,' said Richard, 'I gave it to Sultaniuc.'

'You what? I don't believe you Richard! Whatever next?'

Old General Stravat was doubtful about the whole incident. 'I think you might have lied Richard,' he said.

Young Josif looked across at Richard and smiled sweetly, 'No it wasn't a lie. I think it was an act of love.' Josif's bitterness was slowly melting.

Another week went by and Richard was bothered with severe toothache, but one cure for toothache is good news. Richard received some very good news. Sabina was free. The letter went on to say that she was still confined to the area of Bucharest but that Mihai would soon be allowed to come and visit his father. Richard's breath stuck in his throat.

'Mihai, coming to see me. I won't know him, he was nine when I last saw him. He must be fifteen by now.'

All day and night Richard worried about meeting his

young son again.

'We were so close all these years ago, but what about now, things will have changed.'

One morning Richard sat dreaming about the little boy he had left behind, the strong little Christian who had witnessed to friends and neighbours, strangers and relatives. He remembered the warm little arms that had hugged him tight. Chubby little legs that had struggled up the stairs. Curious little fingers that had pushed open the study door, and the questioning little voice that he had loved to listen to. A sharp voice broke into his dreams.

'Prisoner, your visitor has arrived.'

Richard jumped up, his heart thumping.

Down a corridor and through a door Richard was taken to a row of seats separated from another row of seats by a long row of sturdy iron bars. Richard realised that the visitor opposite would only see a tiny part of his face. He waited, silently, nervous and excited, he could barely sit still. A voice sounded from behind the iron bars, 'Mihai Wurmbrand.'

Richard peered through the bars.

'Where is he, my son? What does he look like?'

A tall thin young man gradually walked along the line of seats until he saw the tired, wrinkled face of his father staring longingly at him from behind the bars. Mihai saw that smile, the blue eyes, it was his daddy.

'Papa!' he whispered and then realising why he was there tried to say as much as he possibly could in two seconds flat.

'Mother says even if you die in prison you must not be sad because we will all meet together in paradise.'

Such cheerful first words, but Richard couldn't help but smile at the young man, his little boy, with the beginnings of his first moustache twitching around his upper lip. Richard didn't know whether to laugh or cry. Pulling himself together he asked after the family.

'How is mother. Have you enough food?'

'Mother is well. Our Father is very rich.'

Richard knew Mihai was talking about God, their heavenly Father.

The guards sniggered as they thought that Mrs. Wurmbrand had remarried and deserted her first husband. But for the rest of the meeting Mihai talked in a sort of religious code.

Richard thought, 'I'm not going to get much family news this way, but it's so good to see him and hear his voice. And they are all well. Praise God.'

As Mihai was escorted out of the prison he shouted to his father, 'I'll see you soon Papa.'

Mihai was amongst the last visitors allowed into the jail. Restrictions were fully restored. No letters, no parcels, no visits!

* * *

Richard sat and relived every moment of his meeting with Mihai. Every word, every smile. Josif came back into the cell, excitedly chattering to one of his cell mates. He had some good news too.

'I'm to be released! I'm going home.'

Richard walked over to his young friend and gave him a great big hug. 'Congratulations Josif!' Josif spent the rest of the day smiling from ear to ear. As a parting gift Richard tore out the lining of his old jacket and gave the warm tweed to his young friend.

'Here, Josif, take this with you to keep you warm.'

Josif's smile grew past his ears! He couldn't believe his luck.

That evening the bread rations were handed round the prisoners and the usual arguments broke out about who had the biggest slice of bread. One of the prisoners looked at Richard's slice. 'The pastor has a far larger slice of bread than me,' he whined. Richard turned and smiled, 'I'm sorry, I know how hungry you are, please take my slice as well.' The prisoner grabbed it and rushed off to the other end of the room to stuff both pieces down his throat.

That night Josif turned and whispered to Richard, 'You've been going through the Bible with me, telling me about Jesus doing this and that, healing the sick, raising the dead, but still I would like to know what he was really like. As a man, what was he like to know?'

Richard's eyes twinkled. 'I knew this old pastor in Room 4. He gave away everything he had, his last piece of bread, his medicine, the coat from his back. I have given away these things sometimes, even when I wanted them for myself. But at other times when men were hungry and sick and in need I could be very quiet and acted as if I didn't care. This other pastor was really Christ- like. I felt sometimes that if I could touch his hand it would heal and calm. One day a prisoner asked him, "What is Jesus like?" In a moment of great courage, he simply and humbly said, "Jesus is like me." The prisoner turned to the old pastor and said, "If Jesus is like you, then I love him."'

'Pastor, if Jesus is like you then I love him too.' Josif smiled, and there was an innocence and peace in his gaze.

'What's that noise?' asked Popp as he turned the corner. Richard and he had just returned from another of their daily chats in the courtyard. But just as they had been ushered back in the door a dreadful groaning was heard from outside one of the other cells.

'It sounds like someone is in a lot of pain.'

Richard turned the corner and was met by a pile of rags, lying crumpled on the floor. The rags moved and Popp gasped, 'Is there someone under all those rags?' Richard gently peeled back some of the blood-soaked shirt and looked into a pair of haunted eyes. It was Boris!

'I don't believe it. When did he come back?' Popp bent down and tried to lift him up.

'OOOHHH! No ... no.'

Richard peeled back some more of the rags and saw what was causing Boris so much pain. His back was congealed with blood and lacerated with scars.

'The other prisoners have attacked him because he is a traitor.'

Just then a crowd of prisoners returned from their exercise and saw Boris lying there. Each one aimed a boot or a fist at him. Richard and Popp got their fair share too.

'Leave me alone Richard. Professor Popp, leave me. I have asked for this...'

A snide remark came from inside one of the cells, '... and you got it too! Traitor!'

Between them Richard and Popp lifted up the pathetic bundle of rags and laid him down on a bed in Room 4.

For the next week they cared for him round the clock, bathing, feeding, soothing, calming and a lot of prayer. Richard sang to him, comforted him with the message of forgiveness. The final night came. Richard lent over to feel Boris' head. Was his temperature any higher? Boris suddenly sat bolt upright and shouted, 'Lord, God, forgive me,' and died.

The following morning an old priest came to Room 4 with his ceremonies and rituals. Richard looked on in disgust. The priest turned on Richard and scolded him.

'Why don't you show a little respect instead of sitting around all the time? This man has just died.'

'Where were you all last week when this man was dying? Did you give him water, did you wash his sores, did you hear him cry? Why is it now that you come along with your ceremonial rituals that meant nothing to him?'

Richard looked on at the meaningless hollow pretence.

The only thing that meant anything was Boris' pure simple cry of, 'Lord, God, forgive me.'

The following morning Richard woke up and said goodbye to Popp. It was time for Richard to move on again. Another prison waited for him. Sergei and Alexi waved through the iron bars of Room 4 shouting, 'Goodbye Richard and thank you!'

Dr. Aldea escorted Richard into the van.

At the station all the prisoners were herded into the wagons. There they lay for hours on end as the train trundled on and on into the countryside.

'How many more prisons will I go to?' asked Richard.

They passed by mountains and rivers, fields and streams. It was a beautiful summer's day.

Free - at last

'Get a move on. Get these chains off them and move them along the line. Hurry up! Move it, move it, move it.'

Richard flinched as the hammer came down on the heavy ankle-chains. It just missed him by a fraction, then he was shoved on down a deep dark corridor. Even on entering the prison Richard could see it was different. The high fortress walls loomed far above them. The 100 year-old walls were cold and thick. Dirt lay everywhere and then suddenly Richard found himself with about twenty others being shoved into a long dark room. Almost immediately a deafening roar greeted them.

'No, get them out. We have no more room. There's no room for them here. Get them out, out, out, out, out!!'

Batons and truncheons beat the new arrivals into the room. Anybody who barred the way got beaten too. Richard tripped over somebody's legs and went flying across the floor. He sat up almost blind in the pitch-dark cell. The smell was overpowering. Urine, sweat, excrement were all over the floor. Straw mouldered in the corner. As Richard's eyesight got used to the surroundings he picked out half-naked men lying on the floor, sprawled over bunks, propped up against walls. There wasn't a spare inch to be had anywhere. If you moved a leg you bumped into someone who would wake up and curse you. Someone else would move an arm and you would get a fist in the face.

Richard coughed in the putrid air. Everyone in the cell gasped for breath. It was a battle just to breathe. Days and nights passed, each one merging into the other, until all you saw was one long night. Richard hated it.

The only chance he got to go out was to take the stinking waste pails out to be emptied. Then he would be back in again. Nobody spoke to him, everyone just lived from one breath to the next. Hundreds of bodies together in a big knot of suffering.

Richard couldn't find a place to stand let alone sit. He had gone to empty the waste bucket and someone had grabbed his space. Richard shuffled to the back of the cell. The air was even more putrid away from the door.

'Everything here aims to give pain. Suffering is our daily bread.'

Richard turned towards the sound of a muffled voice. The voice came out again.

'No sunlight here you see. No windows. It might give us a little hope, sunlight. So it is not permitted. Hope is not allowed.'

'I know all about that. I have been in darkness before. But not like this. Every prison is worse than the last.'

Richard had not yet made out exactly where the voice was coming from. Another shuffle and some straw moved to his left. To start up a conversation he asked the pile of straw, 'How many people are here?'

The voice replied, 'Oh, I don't know. We haven't counted for some time. The numbers change frequently. Anybody taken out that door who isn't holding a waste bucket doesn't return. We've just stopped counting. Some have been in here so long they can't remember how to count.'

Richard moved towards the voice and the moving straw.

'I am Richard Wurmbrand. What is your name?'

'My name no longer matters. If you want to keep your name so be it. But it soon loses its relevance in here. Believe me, you soon won't care that you were ever born – let alone what name you were given.'

Confused. Richard continued, 'Then why are you in here?'

'Why are any of us in here? I believe my son told the secret police that I held political meetings in my kitchen. However, as this is not the case and they did not investigate it any further, I believe I am here because my teenage young Communist son holds a grudge against me. I will return the question dear man – Why then are you in this hole of depravity?'

The bitterness seeped out from the man's heart. Richard could almost feel it in the air he breathed. Taking a deep breath he replied, 'I am a Christian.'

'Oh!' the voice cut in. 'You must be the sort then that really believes and goes around talking about it?'

'Yes, I am. You sound surprised.'

'I am. Because there happens to be rather a lot of you in here at the moment.'

A movement from the other side of the room caught his eye. Richard stared into the gloom. A hand, withered and thin stretched out in his direction.

'Brother, Brother, is it you?'

'I am Richard Wurmbrand.'

'You love the Lord?' The hand shook, trembling as it was raised heavenward in worship.

'Yes, I love the Lord. That is why I am here.'

'You are right.'

A tired, weathered face rose from a bed of soiled rotting straw.

'That is why you are here. The Communists have put you in here because they know their enemy. The truth and light of Jesus Christ. Christ is their enemy. You are his soldier. You are a prisoner of war. But maybe God too has you here for a reason? He has his own purpose.'

As the face smiled in the darkness, the other voice from the other pile of straw muttered something about 'mad Christians and accursed Communists'.

But for Richard it was so good to know he was not alone.

The Church of Christ was still alive – even in this prison cell.

And where two or three are gathered together in Christ's name – Christ is there.

Richard was not alone.

'I am definitely not alone.'

As the weeks went by Richard found himself getting used to the smell and the dark. The prisoners of the long dark cell soon came to know Richard for his excellent stories. Richard soon began a long series of tales about a bandit hero called Pip. Pip was an expert at outsmarting the law. He would hide in his cave during the day and at night he would travel the country looting, robbing and stealing. Richard's listeners sat back enthralled.

'As a young man Pip once entrusted a great deal of money to an innkeeper. On returning from a long journey he asked the innkeeper for his money. Unfortunately the innkeeper had spent it all. In a wild fury Pip stabbed him straight through the heart. Our young friend had to run to the hills to escape and live a life of thievery and murder. Over the years he killed thirty-six innkeepers in a deep rage over his stolen money!'

The listeners oohhed and aahhed at this amazing statistic.

'However,' Richard went on, 'Pip and his band of outlaws soon realised that they were lonely for female company. Pip wanted to take a wife from one of the nearby villages so one night the band of villains ransacked the village and carried off several helpless young girls as prisoners.'

Richard's story then took a different track to the normal bandit story. The girls distracted their kidnappers by telling fantastic tales of adventure, mystery and romance. The girls' stories then ended with one of the girls telling the gospel story and converting all the outlaws including the leader.

One of the prisoners chuckled as Richard finished his story. 'Your stories are like no other stories I have ever heard. The criminal, the victim and the policeman all end up going off to church together! But can you explain this – how did this Jesus of yours turn water into wine? I just don't believe it can be done!'

Before Richard could answer a little old man spoke up in a quiet whispery voice. 'I can't prove that Jesus ever did turn water into wine, but I can tell you how he turned wine into furniture.'

Everybody opened their eyes wide in amazement. What was this amazing miracle they had never heard of? What chapter of the Bible mentioned this?

'When I was a young man I drank every night, beer, spirits, bottles of wine and all sorts of alcohol. I would spend all my money on drink. All my family's money was wasted. My wife did not have enough money to buy food for herself and the children. We did not have one stick of furniture. Then I came to know the Lord Jesus. We became friends, I followed him and stopped drinking. Now my wife has furniture ... that is if the Communists haven't burnt it all by now!' That is how Jesus turned wine into furniture.'

The door opened to the long dark cell and the stories were interrupted by a warden's voice.

'Wurmbrand! You're moving!'

Quickly Richard was ushered out of the cell.

A quiet voice muttered, 'Who will tell us stories now?'

* * *

Richard sat in another cell, with other prisoners. It was tiring, all the shifting about. You settled in with one lot of men, then you had to start again with another lot.

An old farmer reached over to Richard and nudged him on the arm.

'We have a good Doctor here.' And that was it. He didn't say any more. Richard was soon introduced to the doctor. Dr. Marina. All the prisoners loved her. She was young, fresh out of medical school and she still had compassion. Richard and other Christians in the cell immediately started to pray for her conversion.

The old farmer leaned over and nudged Richard on the arm. 'I hear we might be allowed visitors,' and that was all he said. You didn't get much out of the old guy but what he did say was usually very important. He was also right as later on that afternoon Richard heard that he would be allowed a visit the following morning from Sabina! Almost every prisoner in the cell had received the same news. The atmosphere was charged with emotions. Some prisoners, however, would never see their loved ones again. Some had died, others were in prisons or labour camps. Some wives had divorced their husbands and married again. Richard was ecstatic one moment and near to tears the next.

'Sabina!' he would whisper to himself as the night wind blew through the trees. 'Sabina!' Richard's first thought as he woke the next morning. 'Oh Lord, I haven't seen her in eight years.' The doors opened and Richard was marched into the waiting-room. There she was, Richard almost forgot to breathe with the sheer joy of it all. Twenty yards was all that separated them, but it was far enough when all Richard wanted to do was hold her in his arms.

'The pain and suffering has given her a new peace. My beautiful wife.' Richard gripped the small table he stood behind and shouted down the twenty yards.

'Are you all well at home?'

'Yes, we are all well, thank God.'

A guard shouted, 'You are not allowed to mention God here.'

Richard continued, 'My mother, is she still alive?'

'Praise God, she is alive.'

The guard shouted louder, 'I HAVE TOLD YOU THAT YOU ARE NOT ALLOWED TO MENTION GOD.'

Sabina took a deep breath then asked, 'Richard, how is your health?'

Coughing slightly, Richard replied, 'I am in Prison Hospital...'

The guard's voice interrupted again, 'You are not allowed to say where you are in prison.'

Richard tried again, 'Have they mentioned my trial, is there a chance for an appeal?'

'You are not allowed to discuss your trial!'

Richard sighed. 'Sabina, darling, you had better go home. They will not allow us to talk.'

Sabina turned and picked up a basket of provisions to give to Richard. But she was roughly marched straight out of the room. Richard never received even an apple!

That evening Dr. Marina looked at the sad face that stared out the cell window. 'Oh Richard, I had hoped your wife's visit would have helped you. Come along, the prison authorities have given me a surgery! You shall be my first official surgery patient.' Marina opened the door to the new surgery which was small but clean. Richard decided that now would be a good time to preach – out of the earshot of any Communists.

'Dr. Marina, today is the day of Pentecost.'

'Oh yes? And what is that?' Marina looked puzzled as she listened to Richard's heart. 'Breathe deeply, in, out, in, out.'

Richard went on. 'It is the day when God gave us the ten commandments, thousands of years ago.' Suddenly a prison guard appeared from round the corner. Quickly Richard changed his subject. 'When I breathe, Dr. Marina, it hurts me just here.' Richard pointed to his chest. Dr. Marina gave him another puzzled look but investigated the spot anyway. The guard came into the surgery, picked up a file and left.

Richard carried on, '... anyway Pentecost is also the day when the Holy Spirit came to the apostles.' Suddenly, more footsteps. Richard stopped and complained loudly, '... and at night when I sleep, my back is so sore, it wakes me up. The pain is just awful, Dr. Marina.' Marina's mouth twitched with a smile. She realised what Richard was up to. The guard left again with another file. Richard started up again. The next hour was spent sharing the gospel story with the young doctor.

Weeks were spent like this with Richard and Marina sitting together in the examination room. One listening to the gospel story and another listening out for the guards and preaching at the same time. Marina accepted Christ gladly – and was now an even greater ally for the prisoners. Nothing would stop her. Risks were there to be taken and she took them to help the men.

One warm spring evening Richard sat with the old farmer. They both looked out the window, quiet, saying nothing, as usual. Then the old farmer nudged him on the arm. He was quite excited. 'Look, pastor, look.'

Richard turned to look at a swallow's nest perched on the edge of the window.

'Some chicks have just hatched in there. I have just this minute heard their cheeps. The parents are flying to and fro with all the worms their beaks can carry. Do you see pastor, do you see?'

The farmer smiled over their little secret. Turning to Richard he whispered, 'Do you know, they will fly in twenty-one days.'

Richard decided to count. This big outburst from the farmer was amazing in itself, but if what he said was true Richard would be even more amazed. One, two, six, eight, twelve, eighteen, nineteen, twenty, twenty one days and they flew. Richard couldn't believe it!

'God must have arranged their schedule. If he can do that for these little birds he'll do the same for me. Maybe in twenty-one days I will be home.' But the thought brought a touch of sadness to Richard's face. 'I have missed so much. What use will a sick old man like me be to Sabina and Mihai? I will be a burden to them.'

However, a few weeks later a warden came to escort Richard to the interrogation room.

'Wurmbrand, you are free to go.' Papers were signed, forms filled and Richard Wurmbrand was kicked out the door, rags and all.

Going Home

The old man stood on the pavement staring at his feet, not sure what had happened or where he was or anything.

A bunch of young girls stared at him from across the street and giggled when he waved back at them. It had been on a day like this that the nightmare had began.

He took a step.

The sun had shone, a gentle breeze had been blowing on that day.

The old man stopped and listened, insects buzzing, children singing, sounds from a market place not that far away.

A mother shouted to her young son, 'Emil! Keep that shirt clean!'

Another step into the real world.

He walked on. A long wide road stretched ahead into deep lush green. Cows snuffled around the roots of an old chestnut tree. The stillness of it all. It was almost frightening. The old man remembered that feeling. Fear was familiar. He was used to it. He remembered that time long ago. His feet had stepped out quickly that day. His shoes hitting the cracked paving stones. He'd had a coat then. What day was this? He didn't even know.

Richard Wurmbrand, released by the People's Government of Romania.

* * *

Richard was stunned. His senses faced overload as he

wandered on down the white road, on, on, on into the beautiful meadow.

'Look at that leaf now, so perfect, so green. I am touching it, feeling the smoothness of it and there is no voice to shout at me – "Prisoner, get back to work!"'

Richard moved on, 'Flowers, blossoms, green, green grass... Oh! People!' Richard stopped and stared transfixed. Real people, free people, respectable. He looked at his rags and blushed a little, but the old couple came towards him, one holding out a handful of pennies. 'Have you come from there?' The gnarled old hand pointed in the direction of the prison. Richard nodded, and the old man gently pressed the coins into his hand.

'Please, give me your address so that I can repay you?'

But the old couple shook their heads and they went on their way.

Richard walked on, the road he was on would take him into the centre of town from where he would find his way home.

'Home! Home?' Richard was frightened about waking up from this beautiful dream.

Another woman rushed up to him. Pointing in the direction of the prison she asked, 'Have you just come from there?' Richard nodded. The woman pressed some change into his hand. 'For your tram fare.'

'There is no need, I have some money here, look?'

'Please take it, for our Lord's sake.' Then she was gone.

Trams beetled up and down the busy streets of Bucharest. Richard wandered down peering in shop-windows, staring at market stalls. 'Strawberries are in season.' Richard looked at all the beautiful fruits laid out on the shelves.

'Ah, this is where I get my tram.' Crowds soon gathered at the tram stop and smiled and congratulated him. Others asked after friends and relatives.

'My husband was arrested last March, we haven't heard from him. His name is Radu Iova.'

'Have you heard of my daughter, Sophia Valescu? She was arrested in June last year.'

'My husband has been sentenced to twenty years hard labour.'

'I haven't seen my mother in five years.'

'My boyfriend was at the Canal. We haven't heard from him in over two years.'

Every man, woman and child knew of someone in prison. Richard was treated like a conquering hero.

The tram conductor got a big cheer from the crowd when he allowed Richard on free of charge.

'You deserve it mate!' he said vigorously shaking Richard's hand.

As the tram began to move off a voice shouted out, 'STOP, STOP!'

Richard's heart missed a beat. 'It's all a mistake, they have come back for me. They are going to take me back. It's all been a cruel joke.'

But the doors opened and a plump old lady rushed on to the tram with a huge basket of strawberries.

'Oh, thank you, driver. I thought I'd missed it. Phew!' She plonked herself down next to Richard. 'I had to run that last bit. I'm always late for my tram you know! I never learn. I should check the times, I know, but I just forget.' She prattled on and then stopped mid-sentence. Her mouth dropped open as she stared at Richard's clothes. Then she followed Richard's eyes to the mound of strawberries on her lap. 'When did you last taste these?'

Richard thought, 'Not for eight years.'

With that she put her plump little hands straight into the basket and gave Richard a fistful of fat juicy strawberries.

Richard thanked her, his mouth so full of strawberries he could hardly speak.

'Don't mention it,' she smiled. Her eyes misted as her thoughts wandered elsewhere. 'I'd like to think of some woman giving little Michael strawberries ... if he ever gets out.'

The tram slowed to a halt and Richard looked out the window. Rubbing the strawberry juice from off his chin he shouted to the driver, 'That's my stop!'

'Right then, sir. Welcome home.'

Richard jumped out the door and turned to wave to all the well-wishers who were smiling and cheering as the tram whirred its way on into town. The faces in the tram looked on until the old man could be seen no more. Then they turned their faces forward. Many had tears in their eyes as they thought about their own loved ones – 'Will he ever get out?' 'Will we ever see her again?' 'What has happened to mother?' 'Our Father, which art in heaven, look after little Michael...'

Richard stood shaking, home at last, but nervous to even open his own front door. Standing silently he could hear muffled sounds from inside. 'A woman's voice, Sabina! A man's voice? Mihai!!'

'I wonder if that moustache is any thicker? Richard – go through the door and find out? But they're not expecting me! It's your home, your wife, your son! My son – eighteen years old now! Yes, but still your son!'

Richard reached and turned the knob on the door. The door creaked, one step and he was home.

A crowd of young people stood in the hall and stared at the ragged old man who stood there in Mihai's doorway. A young girl with long blonde hair gasped and turned to the young man with the moustache, 'Who on earth, Mihai?' Mihai's face said it all and then he shouted out, 'FATHER!' The gawky young man ran towards the bundle of rags and bones.

Sabina heard Mihai shout and flew out of the kitchen. Richard held Sabina in his arms. Before he kissed her his thoughts went back to his friends, the men he left behind, the Christians who still suffered. He thought about the times they had prayed together, wept together, fought together, laughed together. Richard whispered tenderly in Sabina's ear, 'Don't think that I have come from misery to happiness. I have come from the joy of being with Christ in prison, to the joy of being with him in my family.'

Richard said no more and kissed her.

Re-arrest

Churches were being closed down or converted to clubs, museums or grain-stores. It was the new seven-year plan of the Romanian government. Richard realised that he could not compromise with the Communist government and that sooner or later he would be re-arrested. He fervently hoped that it would be later.

One evening after supper Richard and Sabina knelt and prayed together. Richard opened his heart and laid everything before the Lord.

'Oh Lord, if you know of men in prison whom I can help, of souls that I can bring to you, Lord send me back and I will bear it willingly.'

Sabina paused for a moment and then said, 'Amen.' An inner joy glowed out. They both knew they would serve the Lord more fully, soon.

They came at 1 am., January 5 1959. The doorbell rang, cutting the night peace to shreds, jarring everyone in the house from their sleep. Soon leather boots and metal studs thundered up the stairs. Cupboards were flung open, clothes thrown on the floor, pockets checked, drawers opened, papers confiscated. Mihai was thrown out of his bed and the attic room was scoured from top to bottom. Mihai smiled as he saw a belt of his peeking out from behind a dislodged cupboard.

'And they say that the Secret Police are useless. I have been looking everywhere for that!'

* * *

The black car waited outside. The prisoner was pushed inside, then squashed up between two dark-suited officers. The familiar process once more. The screeching tyres, the violent turns, the mad dash through Bucharest, slamming brakes, the prisoner is thrown out onto the cobbled courtyard of yet another prison.

But it wasn't long before Richard's prayer was answered.

'My father was a drunkard and disappeared with the family savings.'

Richard listened intently. The tired old prisoner had been carrying a burden and he needed to let go. The burden was dragging him down. 'I joined the fascists because they had a cool uniform, some real good marching songs and all the girls loved them. When the Communists came to power they threw me in jail. But they said that if I beat the other prisoners I would earn my release. I believed them. So I ... I ... did it. Now I am sentenced to death, though I was only obeying orders. But I deserve it, I really do...'

Richard saw the guilt and was determined to banish it. 'Man is a sinner, but Jesus has taken the punishment you deserve. There is no need for you to carry all this troubled baggage around with you. Just accept what Jesus is freely offering you – forgiveness.'

Richard spent ten evenings carefully introducing his new friend to Jesus. On the tenth evening Richard's new friend had another friend, the Lord Jesus Christ.

Not all the prisoners were so understanding. Richard would often start to preach and be shouted down by a crowd of very bitter men. They could not stand the pain of his words pricking at their conscience. One evening

Richard sat in a corner and began to speak quietly to a few men gathered round him, but soon a big circle of angry voices and flying fists made for Richard and beat him up right there in the middle of the cell. Boots in his back, fists in the groin, Richard was doubled over, bleeding from his top lip, missing a couple of teeth. A guard shouted through the door and the men fled.

Quickly the wardens rushed in, dragged Richard out and took him to the interrogation room.

'Wurmbrand, who did this?'

Richard said nothing.

'Wurmbrand, tell us, who did this?'

Richard whispered, 'As a Christian, I love and forgive my enemies.'

'Crazy monk,' muttered a guard, 'give him thirty lashes.'

That night, as Richard lay down on his bunk, his back was in agony. Blood seeped through his clothing on to the wooden bench. It left a dark crimson-coloured stain. No-one spoke as he lay his head down and attempted to sleep. From then on Richard was never even interrupted when he spoke. He had earned the right to speak freely. Some of them even listened when he spoke.

Months passed. Richard found himself getting into the routine of punishment, squalor, and boredom. It was especially difficult when he had tasted freedom. Richard knew the thrill of release. Yes, it was very hard, but Richard knew that God had him there for a reason. There was a job to do and Richard was doing it.

'I am God's man in this prison. I will live for him.'

One morning, Richard sat up suddenly, shocked at who he had just seen coming through the door of the cell.

'Popp! I thought you had been released.'

'Richard! I thought you had been released.'

Richard looked at the frail body of his friend, 'Well, it looks as if we are both back.' Richard couldn't believe how ill his friend looked. He moved slowly, rigidly like an old man. Richard held Popp's arm and helped him find a bed next to him. 'Why didn't you answer my letters Popp? I must have written more than twenty.'

Popp's eyes welled up with tears.

'When I left prison, it was as if I went mad with all the freedom. I was afraid that life had passed me by and I wanted to go out and live, live, live. I drank too much beer, spent all my money and left my wife for a younger woman. Then I was sorry, truly sorry. I wanted to speak to you but you were far away.' Popp sniffed, rubbing his nose on his sleeve. 'Then I told everything to another pastor and I blamed it all on the Communists and he went and told them.'

Popp's health got worse and worse, his depression never shifted. Richard tried to cheer him up and one afternoon he introduced him to a friend of his, Pastor Gaston. Gaston's face turned white. Popp just turned away and closed his eyes.

The next day one of the prisoners turned to Popp and insulted him. Popp turned on the prisoner and grabbed him by the throat. Almost immediately the guards came in and beat Popp to the ground. The following morning Popp was dead.

Richard turned to Gaston who looked in the other direction. Gaston was troubled about something. 'Speak to Jesus, he will give you comfort and strength,' Richard said soothingly.

'You speak as if he was here with us, alive,' replied Gaston.

'Of course he is. Don't you believe in the Resurrection?'

Gaston withdrew.

One day both Richard and he were returning from the interrogation room. They had both been given twenty lashes. Gaston turned, 'I want to tell you something Richard, about Popp and the pastor who betrayed him...'

Richard held Gaston's hand. Of course – that was the problem. Gaston had betrayed Popp. Richard had thought there was something wrong. Although Richard loved Popp and missed him, he knew he had to help Gaston. 'Friend, there is no need for you to say any more. I forgive you, Popp would have too if he had known everything. Here, let me tell you about a man who was worse than you.'

Richard sat down on his bunk with Gaston beside him. 'There are only two men my wife kisses, her husband and the man who murdered her family.'

Gaston looked confused. Richard continued.

'When Romania entered the war on Germany's side a programme was started intended to wipe out the Jewish race. Thousands were massacred in one day. My wife, who is a Christian now, comes from a Jewish family. Her family were arrested one morning and taken to a region on the border with Russia. Jews, who were not murdered there, were left to starve. That is where Sabina's family died. When she heard the news of her family's fate she faced it with courage and I have never seen her weep since that day. One evening our landlord came and told us about this awful man staying with him who boasted about the Jews he had killed on the Russian border. My landlord exclaimed I knew this man before the war and he has changed so completely it is as if I don't know him.'

'I was troubled about this and chose not to tell Sabina in case it would distress her. That night I went up to visit with our landlord who introduced me to his guest.'

'Come in Richard, come in, how good to see you. Sabina is well?'

'Yes, she and Mihai are both in bed. I felt like some late-night conversation so I decided to pop in and see you and your guest.'

A large-set man stood up, reaching out to shake my hand.

'A warm welcome to you sir, my name is Richard.'

'Likewise, my name is Borila. It is good to meet one of David's friends.'

The greetings over, I sat down and the social chit-chat began. As the evening wore on Borila relaxed and began to reminisce about the old days. We all listened to the man boast of his killings and murders. 'I killed hundreds at Golta, quite a time I had there. Lots of children, young women – relatively easy in a way, though the little ones were hard to catch sometimes.' Borila chuckled to himself. The old landlord desperately tried to steer the conversation in another direction. Eventually Borila began to talk about another passionate interest of his, music.

'I love to hear the old Ukrainian songs. They are so beautiful and it is so long since I have heard any of them played. It's such a pity there is no piano here.'

'Ah,' I said, 'but there is. We have one in our

apartment downstairs. I suggest that we all take a quick trip down the hall and sing some old Ukrainian songs round my piano. Though we will have to play quietly so as not to wake up Sabina and Mihai. How about it?'

With great excitement Borila and the landlord followed me down the hall. We all converged round the piano. I played all the beautiful old songs, so full of life and feeling. Looking out of the corner of my eye I noticed the landlord's guest humming gently to the melody, swaying from side to side, carried away with the emotion of it all. I had to say something!

'I've something to say to you.' The room was silent, the landlord looked alarmed. The room was tense. Borila looked me in the eye, 'Please speak,' he said.

'If you look through that curtain you can see someone is asleep in the next room. It's my wife, Sabina. Her parents, her sisters, and her twelve-year-old brother were all killed with the rest of her family. You told me you killed hundreds of Jews near Golta, and that is where they were taken. You don't know exactly who you shot so I believe we can assume you killed my wife's family.'

Borila jumped to his feet, his eyes blazing, looking as if he would cheerfully strangle me, right there at the piano. But I just could not shut up. I went on!

'I think I will introduce you to my wife. If I wake my wife up and tell her who you are, and what you have done she will not speak one word of reproach. She will embrace you as if you were her brother, she will bring you supper made from the best things we have in the house. Sabina is a sinner and she will forgive you. Jesus' perfect love can forgive and love you. Only return to him – then everything will be forgiven.'

Borila gasped for air, he held his hand over his chest. His face once red with anger was now pale with fear. I could see the inner man consumed with guilt and misery at what he had done. Borila huddled into a ball, 'Oh God, what shall I do, what shall I do?' Tears ran down his cheeks.

Taking a deep breath I cried out, 'In the name of the Lord Jesus Christ I command the devil of hatred to go out of your soul!' The man trembled and shook asking again and again for forgiveness. 'Lord, I hope and know that you will answer me.'

Then holding his hand I looked him in the eye. 'I said that I would introduce you to my wife.'

Leaving the room I went next door and gently woke Sabina. 'There is a man through in the next room. You must meet him. We believe he murdered your family, but he has repented and now he is our brother.'

Sabina rose and reached for her dressing-gown. She put it on and walked out through the curtain and into the living room. She held out her arms and embraced him. They both wept and Sabina smiled through her tears. Borila lay like a child in her arms and she kissed him. Then she went straight into the kitchen and started preparing a pile of food.

Then I took little Mihai, only two-years-old, out of bed and I placed him in the arms of the new believer. 'See how quietly he sleeps?' I whispered. 'You are also like a newborn child who can rest in his Father's arms. The blood that Jesus shed has cleansed you.'

Borila stayed that night with us. He woke the next morning and, yawning, said, 'It's been a long time since I have slept like that.'

Gaston smiled. 'Thank you Richard.' He reached out and clasped his hand. 'Thank you.'

* * *

'What day is it today?' Richard asked a friend.

'Oh, who knows? Last time I heard it was 1963.'

'1963 eh? How much longer do you think they will keep this up?'

Richard got no reply. The atmosphere in the prison had taken a turn for the worse in the last few months. The prison authorities held conferences and talks where the men were continually reminded of what they were missing on the outside. All prisoners had to attend the Seminars on Communism. Hours would be spent standing listening to more and more lies. Richard sat and tried to soothe his feet.

'Gaston, what are all these loudspeakers doing in the halls?'

'I don't know, someone said there might be a broadcast.'

'Hmm. Do you think we might have some light music to cheer us up?'

Gaston laughed, 'In your dreams!'

Then the speakers crackled into life. Gaston had been right. There was no music to be heard anywhere.

'Communism is good, Communism is good, Communism is good.'

Richard stared out the door, he couldn't even reach the loudspeaker to cover it or knock it off the wall.

Ten minutes passed, 'Communism is good, communism is good, communism is good.'

Half an hour, 'Communism is good, Communism is

169

good, Communism is good.'

Three hours later, 'Communism is good, Communism is good, Communism is good.'

Richard lay back in his bed with his fingers in his ears. 'Communism is good, Communism is good, Communism is good.'

Six hours had passed. Richard couldn't keep his fingers in his ears all the time. 'Communism is good, Communism is good, Communism is good.'

Ten o'clock at night, 'Communism is good, Communism is good, communism is good.'

Three in the morning, 'Communism is good, Communism is good, Communism is good.'

Six in the morning, 'Communism is good, Communism is good, Communism is good.'

Lunch time, 'Communism is good, Communism is good, Communism is good.'

Twenty-four hours brain washing.

Someone screamed, 'How long will this last? I can't stand any more.'

'Be quiet! It will keep going and going until you believe it. Only then will it stop!'

People went mad with it all.

The following day, a play was scheduled for the prison. Of course it wasn't simply to entertain them. The actors got up on the stage and began Act one, Scene one. Mocking Christianity throughout the whole production the guards and officials laughed their heads off. At the end, all the prisoners were told to come up to the front and give their complements concerning the play. 'So well acted.' 'Amazingly funny, I laughed so much.' 'The priest was such an idiot.' 'Best thing I have ever watched.'

It was Richard's turn. Men turned to him as he walked to the front, 'Pastor, I had to say it, I am sorry. It was wrong of me.' 'Forgive me Richard, if I hadn't said it they'd have whipped me.' 'God forgive me.'

Richard stood at the front. 'It is Sunday morning and right now many of our wives and mothers, our sons and daughters are in church praying for us and we have to watch this!'

Tears smeared dirty faces, heads hung in shame.

'Many have spoken out against Jesus, but what have they against him? The Communists are the party of the Workers – Jesus was a carpenter. In fact all that is good in Communism comes from the Christians!' Richard turned and saw the Major glaring at him from across the hall. 'You will be judged too, Major.'

The prisoners burst into cheers, whistles and yells of triumph rang round the hall.

All that Richard earned was a whipping and some news from home. 'Your wife is in jail!' Thrown on to his wooden bench he heard the speakers crackle into life.

'Christianity is stupid, Christianity is stupid, Christianity is stupid. Why not give it up? Why not give it up? Why not give it up? Christianity is stupid, Christianity is stupid, Christianity is stupid. Why not give it up? Nobody believes in Christ now, Nobody believes in Christ now, Nobody believes in Christ now.'

'I DO! I DO! I DO!' shouted Richard.

* * *

'That Wurmbrand is a hard one. Try a different approach with him this time. That idea about leaving him tied up in a blazing-hot room in full summer didn't really work.'

'Yes, we saw that. Torture, whipping, nothing breaks him. What's next then?'

'Take him down to the guard room. I'll meet with him there and discuss a couple of things.'

Richard sat in a clean bright room. It was beautiful.

'Leather armchairs, a desk, flowers. Oh look there's a newspaper. The wallpaper, such colours, I love colours. Oh, it's too much all this beauty.' Richard curled up on his seat and wept. The guard looked on, 'Perhaps he had chosen the right approach after all.'

He stood up and stood over Richard huddled in the chair. 'Look at what you could have if you would just give up Christianity.'

Richard looked straight into the guard's eyes and jumping up he grabbed the newspaper.

'This is printed on the Communist party press, dated 1963. This means 1,963 years since the birth of someone who according to you never even existed. You don't believe in Christ but you have his birthday emblazoned over all your publications!'

Richard returned to his cell. The speakers crackled to life again.

'Christianity is dead. Christianity is dead. Christianity is dead.

Nobody loves you now. Nobody loves you now. Nobody loves you now.

They don't want you any more. They don't want you any more. They don't want you any more.

Christianity is dead. Christianity is dead. Christianity is dead.'

* * *

'Mass-meeting in the hall. Quick march. Out, out, out!!!'

Richard's cell mobilised and marched caterpillar-style down the corridor to the large meeting hall. The Major marched out and stared out at the crowd. He grimaced and almost spat out his words. 'The government has decreed that all political prisoners be released.'

The hall was silent.

'That is all.'

The hall burst into cheers.

Back in the cell they all agreed it was a trick.

* * *

Richard paced up and down his cell humming a little tune to himself. Steel-toed boots marched down the corridor and the door was suddenly opened. 'Wurmbrand, take all your belongings, you're free to go.' Down the hall, through a door, forms and papers and Richard found himself amongst a crowd of other prisoners in the same boat.

'I have been here before,' thought Richard. Looking around he saw many other confused faces. They all seemed to be saying, 'What do we do now?'

A hand patted Richard on the shoulder. 'Brother Wurmbrand!' Richard turned, 'He must be someone from the church?' Smiling he turned to shake his hand, 'How good to see you brother. How are you?'

'Oh well, thank you, now that I am out of prison. In fact I heard a lot about you from your son not so long ago. We shared a cell together.'

Richard's face paled. 'Mihai, in prison. No, not my son, you're mistaken!'

The man looked shocked, 'You didn't know, he has been in jail six years now.'

Richard almost fell to the ground with shock. The man turned and left. Richard felt cold and lonely. The prison commandant strolled past Richard, 'What's it like to have a jailbird for a son?' he laughed. Richard walked away down the road, on, on, on.

'I have to find someone, someone to talk to, someone with a phone. Anyone. Matei and his wife live nearby. I recognise the area.' Eventually finding the street, Richard knocked on several doors before he found them.

'Will I ask them if I can use their phone? If there's nobody at home – there's no point.' But Richard phoned anyway. The bell rang, once, twice, three times. It rang again and again then it went silent. The phone had been lifted up.

'Sabina!' Richard couldn't believe it.

'It's Richard, I thought you were in prison.' There was silence, then a muffled groan at the other end. 'What's happened. Sabina? Are you alright? Sabina!'

Mihai picked up the phone, 'Father, it's all right, Mother's fainted – that's all. Hold on.'

'Mihai, I thought you were in prison?'

'We thought you were dead!'

Richard realised then that it had all been a final Communist trick.

That evening Richard's train trundled into the siding at Bucharest station. Richard looked out the window. Look at all these smiling people with flowers. I wonder who the lucky man is getting this welcome. Wait a minute, there's Anna and Johan, what are they doing here? Why they're waving at me. Maria and her parents! She got home then! Praise the Lord. This welcome – it must be for me. The whole church is here.' Richard pulled

174

down the window and leaned out waving madly. The whole platform cheered wildly! Flowers flew at Richard from every direction. Sabina smiled from the middle of it all.

'I was told you were dead, but I never, never believed it. I will wait for him I said. And now he is here. My husband is home! Welcome home my darling.' And she reached out and kissed him.

* * *

It was a bright breezy Sunday morning. Richard walked along a busy Bucharest street accompanied by a handful of young believers. They were headed for the Zoo. Richard wanted to give them a special treat – something to remember – before he left them.

The visas had come through. Richard, Sabina and Mihai all had authorisation to leave Romania for American shores. 'Not long now,' Richard thought. 'Someone has to tell the Western Christians what is happening here. They have to know, they have to pray!'

A large-throated lion let out a big roar, showing a full set of shiny white teeth. A portion of its dinner sat clenched between a set of shiny white claws.

One youngster turned and laughed, 'Good job it's behind those bars, eh Pastor?' Richard smiled. Then he sighed, 'Your forefathers in the Christian faith were thrown to beasts like these. They died gladly, because they believed in Jesus. The time may come when you also will be imprisoned and suffer for being a Christian. Are you ready to face that day?'

Everyone of them, with tears in their eyes said, 'YES!'

Alone with God

An old man strides out across the city street, his long brown overcoat flapping in the breeze. There is nobody to talk with him this evening. He walks alone. But he talks with God.

'Father, thank you for this beautiful evening. The sunshine, the warmth, the fresh breeze. Thank you for the warmth of your love to me, for the fresh breeze of the Holy Spirit on my heart. Your ways are wonderful.'

He hums quietly to himself. A hymn tune comes to mind as he strides along over the smooth dry paving-stones.

Suddenly, a crowd of young shining faces appears from out of an imposing red doorway. A banner stretched across it says, 'Burgers, Pizza, Hot dogs!' They rush past him with their soft leather sneakers, T-Shirts flapping in the breeze.

'They have freedom of speech, but their lives have no room for God. All they want is fun, money, clothes.'

The old man sighs. He walks on. He was one of them once.

He mutters under his breath,

'I too was a believer in lies. I too thought that a good time was all I ever needed.'

The old man's Sunday shoes stride out again over the smooth dry paving-stones.

A barrage of noise and colour meet him as he passes by the street-stalls. Traders shout out to passers-by trying desperately to sell their last few watches, T-Shirts, bottles of perfume. People shout out to him as he rushes past.

'New in this morning Sir, only the best labels. Your wife will love you for this perfume. It's the best.'

The old man turns and smiles, adding, '... and very, very, expensive? Yes?'

The stallholder pauses, and smiles back. 'Expensive yes, but you will not get better, not in all of Washington, D.C. Even the president's wife wears this stuff.'

The old man smiles as the trader turns away with a 'Have a nice day.'

A young girl strides along the pavement singing about 'Love, love, love!'

The old man turns to her as she crosses the road and quietly but firmly says, 'Jesus loves you.'

'What did you say?'

'Jesus loves you.'

'Yeah, right,' and she walks on.

The Sunday shoes weave in and out avoiding other Sunday shoes going in other directions. Churches close their doors, services over, it is time for lunch.

The old man finally finds what he was looking for.

The monument. It stands there on the wall. A giant plaque with writing skillfully engraved into its stone. The constitution of the United States.

'But if I stand a bit further back, yes, there he is. George Washington.' It was amazing – like an illusion. If you looked at the monument one way you saw the words. If you looked at it from another angle, George Washington appeared – as if by magic.

The old man looks at the amazing piece of architecture. 'I almost didn't see it at first, but then I stepped back and looked again, and there he was. The face behind it all. My life is like that. Behind the prison, behind the pain, behind the suffering, the loneliness, he was always there, the unseen being, keeping me, keeping us all in the faith. Giving me the strength to conquer – my Lord Jesus Christ.'

Richard Wurmbrand, free at last.

THINKING FURTHER TOPICS

1. Arresting Times

Richard was in a country where it was impossible to worship God in public. Do you worship God? Look up the word worship in the dictionary - what does it mean? Write out a list of places you can worship God in... did you realise that you can worship God everywhere? Do you ever think about how fortunate you are to be in a country where you're able to worship God freely?

Thank God that you can pray, read the bible and go to church. Remember to pray for those who cannot do that as easily as you.

2. Prisoner, March!

When Richard was in prison not even his wife knew where he was - but God knew. Read Psalm 139:1-12. Have you ever thought that God sees and knows everything about you? How does that make you feel? Richard found comfort from knowing that God knew everything about him but maybe that makes you feel uncomfortable? Why ? Do you have something to hide?

Remember that God knows that too, so take time to confess what you've done and ask for his forgiveness.

3. Sabina!

Initially Sabina was angry that Richard had become a Christian - how do you think you would cope if you had a similar reaction from friends or family when you became a Christian? But then God showed Sabina the emptiness of all the things she was trying to fill her life with and her need for him.

What do people try and fill their lives with today? They might get some happiness from these things but do you think the happiness really lasts?

Pray for people you know who don't know God - that God would show them how much they need him. Remember that your life will speak to them too.

4. Richard's Guest

Richard was obviously frightened. What things frighten you? Perhaps you worry so much that you feel miserable? Remember that you can tell God about what scares you and that the Bible is full of promises to reassure you. Read these examples: - 1 Peter 5:7, 2 Thessalonians 3:3 and Hebrews 13:6.

Also read Psalm 56:3 and Isaiah 12:2. What does it mean to trust someone? What is it about God that makes him worth trusting? Remember, people might let us down - but God has a proven track record of never letting his people down, so you can have confidence in him and trust him with your future.

5. Questions, Questions

Richard made time to pray to God first thing every day, even in the difficult situation he was in. Do you set aside time for God everyday? It's easy for other things to take over, so make sure you find a specific time each day when you can read your Bible and pray to God. Perhaps you could use a daily study guide to help you understand the Bible passage you read? Maybe you could start a prayer diary to remind you of things/people to pray for and answers to prayer that you've already had?

Patrascanu 'used to pray but gave up' - why do you think he might have done that? How can we make sure we don't just give up praying?

6. Death and Depression

Richard went through a time in prison when everything almost became too much for him to bear. He even considered ending his life but God lifted his spirit through the beauty of creation and the song of a young girl.

Do you ever feel that everything is getting on top of you and you can't cope? Perhaps you're struggling right now or you worry that you won't be strong enough to handle difficult times in the future? Read Psalm 29:11, Psalm 46:1 and 2 Corinthians 12:9-10. Isn't it wonderful to know that even when you're at your weakest and lowest, God's strength is everything you need? You're not alone!

7. Torture

Praying for friends and those we love is easy - but what about praying for our enemies? Richard regularly prayed for the prison guards and those who tortured him. How could he do that, do you think?

Read Matthew 5:44 and Luke 6:35. What do these passages tell us? Think of Jesus himself and how he died for us. Isn't it amazing that Jesus died for you and loved you even when you had no time for him? What can we learn from his example? Remember that God knows how hard it is to love your enemies, so ask him to help you to pray for, and even love, those who aren't easy to love and who make things difficult for you.

8. Solitary Silence

Richard found that being able to recall verses he had memorised brought him a lot of comfort when he didn't have access to a Bible.

Have you ever learnt any Bible verses off by heart? Why not try it? You could start with John 3:16 and John 14:6. If you can learn these, then why not learn a few more? You'll find a time when it will be good to recall a Bible verse to help you along.

Bible verses give us the answers to difficult questions and they can reassure you in a frightening situation or comfort you when you are worried or scared.

9. Dancing and Leaping and Praising God

Richard wrote the name of Jesus on his cell wall and got into a lot of trouble over it. Read Matthew 1:21 to find out why Jesus' name is so special. The commandments teach us that God's name deserves to be honoured and not used in a wrong way - Exodus 20:7.

Often people use God's name without thinking about how great and good God is. They use it as a swearword when they feel angry and annoyed. If you love Jesus, it will hurt you to hear people use God's name in a wrong way. What is the right way to use God's name?

10. Dear Jesus

Richard talks to God by turning his prayers into letters. Why not try that too? It might help you to keep focussed when you pray and you can also look back later and see how God has answered your prayers.

Maria Poppov felt disgraced because she was in prison. Maria felt she'd let everyone down and maybe they would think badly of her. It's easy to condemn others but what should we remember about ourselves before we do that? Read John 8:1-11. How did Jesus respond to the people who condemned the women who had sinned. What can we learn from Jesus' example?

11. Room 4

Even Richard's presence in Room 4 had an impact on the other prisoners - a spiritual atmosphere and brotherly love developed between them. What impact should Christians have on the people they mix with? Read Matthew 5:14-16. Why are Christians to be the light of the world? What does that mean about how we should live?

The atheist in this chapter had spent his life not believing that God existed but then came to trust God just before he died. He left it to the last minute. What are the benefits of becoming a Christian while you're young? Read Ecclesiastes 12:1 and if you haven't done so already, ask Jesus to become your Saviour today !

12. Re-education

Do you find it easy to forgive others? Sometimes we like to hold onto our grudges and remind people of how often they've let us down. Have you ever thought about how often you've sinned against Jesus and let him down? Have you asked him to forgive you? It's amazing to see the abbot in this chapter forgive the young man who had tortured him - how could he do that? Read Matthew 6:12 and Matthew 6:14-15 and ask God to help you to forgive and to stop holding grudges.

Learning to forgive will remove bitterness from your heart and help you to be more like Christ.

13. New Cell, Old Problems

A food parcel arrived for the old General. Rather than keeping it to himself, the General asked Richard to share it out amongst the men. How can we learn to think of others and not just keep things for ourselves? What does the Bible say about it? Read 1 Timothy 6:18-19.

Maybe you just do things to get some recognition? Do you think it matters what your motives are - or is it just enough that you've done something good? Read Luke 16:15 and Colossians 3:23-24 and remember that whatever you're doing, you're doing it for God. He sees your actions and your motives and your reward will come from him.

14. Free - at last

The nest outside the window reminded Richard that God was in control and had planned his life for him, just as he had planned the swallows' schedule. Read Matthew 10:29-31, isn't it amazing to know that God as a care and an interest in the little birds?

Do you sometimes feel that nobody cares? Perhaps you think nobody listens or even notices that you're around? How does that make you feel? Well, you can be certain that God has a care and an interest in you - even the hairs on your head are numbered! Remember, God has a plan for you - read Proverbs 3:5-6. Don't ever be tempted to think that nobody cares - God does, so trust Him!

15. Going Home

After all he'd been through, Richard got home at last and told Sabina, 'Don't think that I have come from misery to happiness. I have come from the joy of being with Christ in prison, to the joy of being with him in my family.' God's presence had been constant through everything! What difference do you think that would have made?

Do you ever think that if you're a Christian then God is constantly with you too? What difference should that make in your life? Thank God for being with you always and pray for those who don't know God yet. Read Matthew 5:16 again and ask God to help you to witness to the people you mix with and to share Jesus with them whenever you can.

16. Re-arrest

In spite of everything he suffered, Richard was willing to go back to prison and be God's man there, if it was God's will. Do you like to choose the easy option in life? Well, God's choice for our life isn't always easy - can you think of some examples? What if we've always wanted to do something but God says 'No'? Why doesn't God's will just fit in with our plans?

Read Isaiah 48:17-18 and remember that God knows what's best for you - so trust his better judgement and be assured that he knows what he's doing!

17. Alone with God

What does it mean to have freedom of speech? Richard and his family make their way to the USA, where they find freedom of speech and freedom to worship but also many people with no room for God in their lives.

Look around you - is it the same where you live? The people around you maybe think they don't need anything and they definitely don't need God - but do they? How can you show them that Jesus isn't just a 'crutch' for old, sick and weak people? What can you do to help to get the message of Jesus through to people who don't see their need of him?

Read 1 Timothy 6:17 and Romans 3:23 and remember that everyone needs Jesus - even if they don't realise it right now. It's never easy to tell people about Jesus Christ. Sometimes we get tongue tied. Sometimes we don't know the right answers. But God knows what it's like.

Pray that he'll help you to share the message of Jesus with those around you. Ask God to help you show your friends that even if they have everything money can buy - they still need Jesus.

My Prayer Diary

The Bible says, 'Devote yourselves to prayer, being watchful and thankful. And pray for us, too' Colossians 4:2-3. Write down the names of those people you want to pray for every day. They may be your family and your special friends.

Write down the names of your minister or church leader and those people who help in church life like Sunday School teachers, Youth workers etc.

Write down names of people who need your prayers i.e. missionaries, or people doing other difficult jobs. They could be people who are old or ill or who are feeling lonely. Write down a person for every day of the week and pray for them each week, on this day. After having read this book let's pray to God about some of the things we have learnt and about specific issues that we've read about.

Government : Pray for the people who make the laws and decisions in your country.

Pray that God will guide them and that they will bring in laws and make decisions which are in line with God's word.

Pray that more Christians will be brought into positions of power in your country.

Remember countries where laws make it very difficult to be a Christian. Pray that God will strengthen his followers in these places and that God will change the hearts of their leaders. Pray for the organisation, Voice of the Martyrs and their work amongst the persecuted church.

Your Country: Pray for your country and the other countries and communities that make up your world.

Remember Christians who are struggling. Pray that they will get encouragement from meeting with other Christians, from the Bible and from prayer.

Pray for those in your country who don't know about Jesus. Pray that they will see how much they need Jesus and find him for themselves.

World Issues: Be informed about your world and nation. Read a newspaper or watch the news and pray about the problems you hear or read about.

Families: Pray for families separated by war, imprisonment, disasters or illness. Pray that they will be safely brought back together. Pray that they will be brought to know Jesus.

Suffering: Pray for those suffering from disease or famine. Thank God for providing for you and don't forget to do what you can for others, through prayer and through giving.

Prison Ministry: Pray for organisations who bring the gospel into prisons. Pray those Christians who visit prisons every week. Pray that they will share the good news of Jesus with the prisoner. Remember Christians who are imprisoned because of their love for Jesus. Ask God to be with them, giving them strength and opportunities to speak up for him. Pray that, if it's God's will, they will get the freedom they deserve.

Postscript

Richard Wurmbrand used his freedom to spread the news about the suffering of Christians under Communism. Inspired by his example, organisations were founded throughout the world with these main purposes:

(1) To encourage and empower Christians to fulfil the Great Commission in areas of the world where they are persecuted for their involvement in propagating the gospel of Jesus Christ. We accomplish this by providing Bibles, literature, radio broadcasts and other forms of aid.

(2) To give relief to the families of Christian martyrs in these areas of the world.

(3) To undertake projects of encouragement, helping believers rebuild their lives and Christian witness in countries that have formerly suffered Communist oppression.

(4) To equip local Christians to win to Christ those who are opposed to the Gospel in countries where believers are actively persecuted for their Christian faith.

(5) To emphasise the fellowship of all believers by informing the world of atrocities committed against Christians and by remembering their courage and faith.

You can receive information about Christians suffering today by writing to:

RELEASE INTERNATIONAL, P.O. Box 19,
Bromley, BR2 9TZ.   UK
Tel: 020 8460 9319   Email: Releaseint@aol.com

VOICE OF THE MARTYRS, P.O. Box 598,
Penrith, NSW 2751, AUSTRALIA.
Tel: 612 4721 8221   Email: thevoice@vom.com.au
Website: www.vom.com.au

VOICE OF THE MARTYRS, P.O. Box 117,
Port Credit, Mississauga ON L5G 4L5, CANADA
Tel: 905 602 4832   Email: thevoice@persecution.com
Website: www.persecution.net

LOVE IN ACTION SOCIETY, P.O. Box 4532
New Delhi 110016, INDIA
Tel: 11 651 7265   Email: jjob@pobox.com

VOICE OF THE MARTYRS, P.O. Box 69-158
Glendene, Auckland 1230, NEW ZEALAND
Tel: 649 837 1589   Email: vomnz@iconz.co.nz

THE VOICE OF THE CHRISTIAN MARTYRS
P.M.B. 21078, Ikeja, Lagos, NIGERIA
Tel: 01 4921291   Email: vcmnige@rcl.nig.com

CHRISTIAN MISSION INTERNATIONAL,
P.O. Box 7157, 1417 Primrose Hill, SOUTH AFRICA
Tel: 11 873 2604   Email: cmi@icon.co.za

VOICE OF THE MARTYRS, P.O. Box 443, Bartlesville
OK 74005-0443, USA
Tel: 918 337 8015   Email: thevoice@vom-usa.org
Website: www.persecution.com

CHRISTIAN FOCUS

Good books with the real message of hope!

Christian Focus Publications publishes biblically-accurate books for adults and children.

If you are looking for quality Bible teaching for children then we have a wide and excellent range of Bible story books - from board books to teenage fiction, we have it covered.

You can also try our new Bible teaching Syllabus for 3-9 year olds and teaching materials for pre-school children.

These children's books are bright, fun and full of biblical truth, an ideal way to help children discover Jesus Christ for themselves. Our aim is to help children find out about God and get them enthusiastic about reading the Bible, now and later in their life.

Find us at our web page:
www.christianfocus.com